Praise For Crystal Grids Power

"A very well written and easy to understand guide with very complete procedures. The Sacred Geometries used for the grids are well defined. Ethan discusses that not only intention is required but also positivity, focus, action and effort. Ethan has also addressed the direction of the energy flow, which is quite important for gridding if one desires results. The entire book is highly recommended for all!"

-Melody, author of the Love Is In The Earth series

Spiritual Book Awards Finalist

Crystal Grids Power was chosen as a top three finalist in Soul & Spirit Magazine's Spiritual Book Awards 2018 for Best Crystals Book.

Copyright © 2017 Ethan Lazzerini

All rights reserved

1st Edition

Printed by CreateSpace

Book cover, diagrams and illustrations are copyright of

Ethan Lazzerini

No part of this book may be reproduced, stored in a retrieval system, or transmitted in any form or by any means, electronic, photographic, mechanical, photocopying or recording, other than for 'fair use' as brief quotations embodied in articles and reviews, without prior written permission of the copyright holder.

The information and advice contained in this book is in no way to be considered a substitute for consultation with licensed medical practitioners. The metaphysical information is based on the author's personal experience, beliefs and research. Results will vary for everyone and are not guaranteed. Always use common sense with spiritual information and crystals. Any use of the information in this book is at the reader's own discretion and risk.

Please note the printable template document is offered as a free gift and not included in the price of this book. This offer is subject to availability and may be removed at any time without notice. There is no guarantee it will be available in the future.

ISBN: 1542827558
ISBN-13: 978-1542827553

CRYSTAL GRIDS
POWER

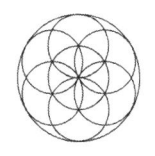

Harness The Power of Crystals
& Sacred Geometry for Manifesting
Abundance, Healing & Protection

ETHAN LAZZERINI

ALSO BY ETHAN LAZZERINI

Psychic Protection Crystals
The Modern Guide To Psychic Self-Defence With Crystals For Empaths & Highly Sensitive People

Crystal Healing For The Chakras
A Beginner's Guide To The Chakras & Chakra Balancing With Crystals

Dedication

This book is dedicated to all those who have supported me and patiently waited for the release of this book. To the valued readers of my blog articles and books. Old friends and new, you know who you are. Thank you for your kind words and being as passionate about crystals as I am. I give you my heartfelt gratitude.

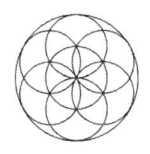

CONTENTS

Introduction.. i

1. The History & Origins of Crystal Grids....... 1

2. How Crystals Grids Work............................ 9

3. Sacred Geometry Reference Guide.............. 19

4. Crystal Grid Tools & Essentials................... 37

5. How To Prepare Your Crystal Grid............. 51

6. Crystal Grid Care & Maintenance................ 65

7. Enhancing Your Intentions........................... 73

8. Simple Crystal Grids.................................... 83

    Simple Abundance Crystal Grid.................. 86

    Simple Healing Crystal Grid....................... 88

    Simple Protection Crystal Grid................... 90

    Simple Relationships Crystal Grid.............. 92

9. More Advanced Crystal Grids..................... 95

    Abundance & Prosperity Crystal Grid......... 96

All Purpose Crystal Grid...........................	98
Angelic Connection Crystal Grid...............	100
Attract A Loving Partner Crystal Grid.......	102
Aura Balancing Crystal Grid......................	104
Aura Clearing Crystal Grid........................	106
Cleanse Home Crystal Grid.......................	108
Confidence & Courage Crystal Grid..........	110
Earth Healing Crystal Grid........................	112
Faith & Hope Crystal Grid........................	114
Healing Crystal Grid..................................	116
Home Blessing Crystal Grid......................	118
Home Protection Crystal Grid...................	120
Increased Energy Crystal Grid...................	122
Inspiration & Ideas Crystal Grid................	124
Karma Release Crystal Grid......................	126
Life Purpose Crystal Grid..........................	128
Motivation Crystal Grid.............................	130
New Beginnings Crystal Grid....................	132
Overcome Obstacles Crystal Grid.............	134
Peace & Harmony Crystal Grid.................	136

Personal Healing Crystal Grid.................... 138

Protection Crystal Grid.............................. 140

Psychic Attack Shield Crystal Grid........... 142

Psychic Development Crystal Grid........... 144

Self Love Crystal Grid............................... 146

Sleep Well Crystal Grid............................. 148

Spiritual Guidance Crystal Grid................. 150

Stress Relief Crystal Grid.......................... 152

Success Crystal Grid.................................. 154

10. Creating Your Own Crystal Grids............... 157

11. Troubleshooting... 165

Afterwards.. 173

About The Author... 174

Bibliography.. 175

INTRODUCTION

I first learned about Crystal Grids many years ago. There was very little information about them back then or it was hard to find. Over the years and perhaps thanks to the Internet, this has now changed. The interest and popularity of Crystal Grids has continued to grow, especially in recent years.

One of the first Crystal Grids I ever made was put around my whole bedroom to help create a peaceful environment conducive to sleep. It worked, but how?

As I looked at the Crystal Grids others had created, I noticed that there was still a veil of mystery about them. Many sources did not say why they used each different type of crystal in the grid. Even when they did, they never seemed to explain the significance of the geometric arrangement of the stones.

That's why it's so important for me to explain to you exactly why I selected the crystals in these grids and why I chose the geometric shapes that I did. I think it's important to understand not only what you're doing but also why you're doing it. This book will help you understand the metaphysical mechanics and remove the mystery and secrecy behind Crystal Grids.

The Crystal Grids in this book were not created just to look pretty. I have carefully researched and formulated these Crystal Grids using Sacred Geometry, combined with my knowledge of crystals. I have made sure that they will be practical and helpful tools to use in all areas of your life.

How To Use This Book

Please make sure you read through this book in order to make sure you understand things fully before using any grids. It was written like a course, with each chapter building on the next. Even if you have worked with Crystal Grids before you are going to be learning new things here. **The printable Crystal Grid Templates link is given later in the book for this reason.**

You are going to learn how to harness the energies of crystals and Sacred Geometry to amplify your intentions, focus your mind and manifest positive change. But first we will explore the origins and historic influences behind the Crystal Grids used today. You will discover the connection between Sacred Geometry and crystals and why they form the powerful blueprint behind Crystal Grids.

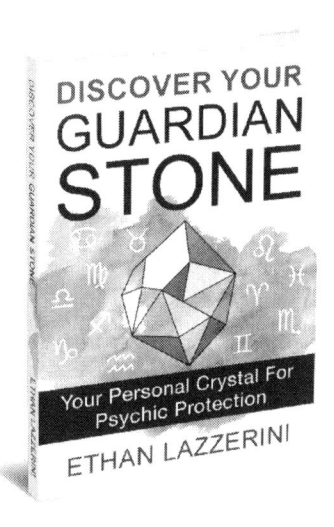

Before we begin I just want to let you know about a free gift I have for anyone who subscribes to my Crystal Newsletter and updates. Once you join you can download my free Ebook **Discover Your Guardian Stone**. This book was written to help you find your personal protection crystal using astrology.

If you're interested please visit my website or go directly to the link below:

www.ethanlazzerini.com/freegift

CRYSTAL GRIDS POWER

ETHAN LAZZERINI

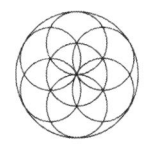

1

THE HISTORY & ORIGINS OF CRYSTAL GRIDS

Some have said that Crystal Grids are an ancient tradition while others say they are a modern invention. So which is true? It is hard to pinpoint exactly when and where the first Crystal Grid was made.

Crystal Grids also known as Crystal Nets or Crystal Layouts, appear to have developed during the growth of modern day Crystal Healing. This began sometime around or after the early 1980's. Just like the practice of Crystal Healing today, Crystal Grids draw on ancient knowledge, traditions and beliefs.

There is plenty of evidence of the meaningful placement of stones and crystals in several different cultures and eras. This might be where the idea came from, or at least Crystal Grids follow a similar system. In this chapter we will explore a few of these ancient spiritual practices in more detail.

Stone Circles & Standing Stones

Megalithic monuments can be found all around the world. The Stone Circles and structures of Europe are well known, truly ancient, yet still shrouded in mystery and controversy. The makers of these structures clearly believed in the importance of using stones, their position on the landscape and their relation to the Sun, Moon and very likely the Stars.

It is believed that places like this were once used for spiritual practices, rituals and healing. Esoteric and metaphysical beliefs about these standing stones say that the ancients were tapping into the energy of the Planet. Or that they were drawing in energies from the Cosmos. These locations are said to have been built on places of importance. This includes Ley Lines and Vortex points, which form where Ley Lines converge. This network of energy that crosses the landscape is closely connected to Sacred Geometry.

What we do know is that these standing stones are placed with geometric design and alignment to other important monuments. They are also placed to align with the Sun, Planetary cycles and the constellations.

Stonehenge is one of the most well known Stone Circles in the world. The larger stones were somehow transported to England from a mountainous region in Wales. Preseli Bluestone seems to have had some kind of special meaning for these people. The circular markings it has may have represented the stars or the Universe itself.

Perhaps these standing stones linked heaven and Earth in some way? Their original purpose may have been lost in the mists of time, but there was clearly a deeply meaningful intention behind the placement of these stones.

The Breastplate of the High Priest

The Breastplate of the High Priest is a curious and sacred garment, which is mentioned in the Bible. Specific instructions are given on the gemstones to use, their position and geometrical arrangement:

"And you shall make a breastplate of judgment, in skilled work; like the work of Ephod you shall make it; of Gold, blue and purple and scarlet stuff, and fine twined linen shall you make it. It shall be square and double, a span its length and span its breadth. And you shall set in it four rows of stones. A row of Sardius, Topaz and Carbuncle shall be the first row; and the second row an Emerald, a Sapphire, a Diamond; and the third row a Ligure, an Agate and an Amethyst; and the fourth row a Beryl, an Onyx and a Jasper" – Exodus 28:15-21

The text then goes on to say that the stones represent the twelve tribes of Israel. As with any ancient text the names of the gemstones are hard to translate and opinions vary on quite a few of them. In the first century AD, the Jewish historian Flavius Josephus said that the stones also represented the months of the year and signs of the Zodiac. This astrological connection later became associated with the tradition of Birth Stones in jewellery.

It is significant that there are twelve stones in the breastplate. This number occurs frequently across cultures as having religious or mystical meaning. The stones are arranged in four rows of three, which could signify the four seasons of three months. Or the four elements associated with the signs of the Zodiac.

What we do know is that these crystals were considered to have some kind of holy and symbolic power. They were stones that represented tribes and possibly monthly cycles or astrological constellations.

Mandalas

Although mandalas do not require the use of crystals, they are connected to the use of Crystal Grids. The word mandala originates from an ancient Sanskrit word meaning 'circle'. A mandala may also incorporate other shapes. Mandalas are found in both the Hindu and Buddhist traditions and go back thousands of years. They are said to represent the Universe, displaying sections of the Physical and Spiritual Worlds.

Buddhist Monks are trained to create these mandalas using coloured sand, which does naturally contain Quartz. Sometimes powdered crystals or gemstone beads are used. The creation of the mandalas is a form of focused meditation practice. After the mandala has been created it is destroyed. This represents the temporal nature and illusion of time and space.

Medicine Wheels

The Medicine Wheel originates from the Native American tribes. These wheels are created from stones arranged in a circular pattern with spokes or a cross inside. There is also usually a stone placed at the centre of the circle.

The designs are a symbol of the Native American traditional beliefs and spirituality. Different spokes and sections of a Medicine Wheel may represent and align with the compass points or the rising and setting of the Sun. They may also symbolise the seasons or elements. Some Medicine Wheels are large historic stone monuments similar to Stone Circles, which are aligned with the four cardinal directions. A few are associated with alignments to the Moon, Stars and Planets.

Like a mandala, many feel the creation of a Medicine Wheel is a form of meditation. In ancient times the large Medicine Wheels may have operated as a communal site for traditional teachings, spiritual knowledge and divine connection.

Crystal Grids Today

So what we can see is that the idea of arranging stones into a symbolic geometric pattern has been used since prehistoric times. Crystal Grids are quite possibly a development of these ancient structures, ideas and traditions.

Modern Crystal Grids draw on the wisdom of Sacred Geometry, metaphysical beliefs and Crystal Healing traditions. You could see them more as a spiritual technology, which I have no doubt will continue to grow and evolve. There are already several different types of Crystal Grids that can be clearly defined. These include the following:

Regular Crystal Grids

This is the most well known and popular type of Crystal Grid used today. The crystals are arranged into small or medium sized geometric patterns on a flat surface for many different purposes. Regular Crystal Grids like these are often used for things like manifesting, psychic protection, healing or support during difficult life changes. They can be made for yourself or to help others. You can also use a Crystal Grid template for these.

Location Crystal Grids

This is a large Crystal Grid, which is placed around a room, building, garden or within the landscape. These grids are usually created to change, maintain or protect the energy of a place. Location Crystal Grids can be temporary such as a grid within a bedroom for sleep troubles. Or they can be permanent such as crystals left buried in the earth. Crystals could be placed at the four corners of a House for protection. A Crystal Grid could be made outside in nature, to create a sacred space for meditation.

Body Crystal Grids

This is a Crystal Grid that is placed on or around a person. These are temporary Crystal Grids, which are used in Crystal Healing work or for Psychic Protection for example. The crystals are placed to change the energy within the Aura and Chakras. You could use a Crystal Grid to cleanse or balance the Aura. Or crystals could be placed around the body for grounding.

In this book we will be mostly looking at the first type of Crystal Grid, as it is the most useful and versatile. I have also included several really helpful Location Crystal Grids and Body Crystal Grid layouts for you to try as well.

ETHAN LAZZERINI

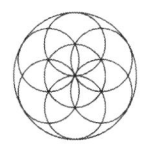

2

HOW CRYSTAL GRIDS WORK

Crystal Grids may not be the most simple way to use crystals, but they can be very effective. This is the reason more and more people are working with them. Later on I will show you step by step how to make both simple and more complex grids for yourself and others. But first we are going to explore how and why these arrangements of crystals work.

Crystal Grids combine the energies and properties of specific crystals with the mechanics of other metaphysical systems. This is all done with the intention of creating a desired result. What this means is that the energy of the crystals is focused, directed and amplified when used within a Crystal Grid.

The building blocks of all Crystal Grids are the crystals themselves. So let's start with the essential part of all Crystal Grids before we explore the other aspects. Please note that throughout this book I refer to the words crystal and stone interchangeably to include any mineral or gemstone.

Crystals & Crystal Healing

Crystals have long been used for their therapeutic, spiritual or healing properties. What we now call Crystal Healing or Crystal Therapy today is the development of these ideas and traditional beliefs in modern times.

From a scientific point of view, crystals contain various combinations of minerals and have their own electromagnetic field. When we look at most crystals close up under high magnification we see they have a crystalline structure, which is geometric. This exists at a microscopic level and repeats throughout the whole crystal. Some crystals grow into clearly geometric formations such as Quartz, Amethyst, Pyrite and Fluorite to name but a few.

These fascinating geometries, energy fields, repeating patterns and structures all seem to add weight to the metaphysical belief that crystals emit and store energies or information. As for the source of their manifesting properties, when you think about it crystals are creative energy in physical form. The minerals that created these crystals came from ancient Stars and Planets as they were still forming. Many crystals are thousands if not millions of years old. Some grew billions of years ago and are older than all life on Earth.

Crystals contain elements that are a fundamental part of all life on Earth, such as Iron and Silica. Crystals are crystallised seeds of creative energy. The alchemical process that created these crystals deep within Earth's fiery furnace, can be tapped into for manifestation work.

From the spiritual point of view, crystals also act as catalysts. They alter the vibration of energies around you or within you, to create change in your life. They can be programmed for specific needs and desires. The crystals that are used in a Crystal Grid are selected to carry the types of energies needed for a situation. They can be seen as the power source or batteries of a Crystal Grid. Some crystals are used to amplify or broadcast these energies out into the Universe or towards a person or place.

Even the forms of crystals used such as Crystal Points, Double Terminated Crystals or Crystal Pyramids all have their own purpose and way of directing energies. We will be looking at this in more detail later on.

The physical structure of the crystal also acts as an anchor point for energies. The Crystal Grid becomes a physical yet symbolic representation of the intention behind it. This structure also acts as a visual reminder of the purpose behind the grid. It speaks to us both consciously and at a subconscious level.

Sacred Geometry

Sacred Geometry is the belief in the spiritual or divine significance and power of geometry. These geometric shapes, which exist everywhere from our cells to the Galaxies, are seen to represent the fingerprint of the divine. They are like the framework for creation and all life. Without geometry there would be no manifested world or life forms.

In recent years Sacred Geometry has become more and more explored outside of esoteric groups. This subject is vast and encompasses ancient cultures, traditions, religions, architecture, genetics, biology, physics, astrophysics, spirituality, cosmology, numerology and philosophy. Hundreds of books have been written about it and whole volumes could be written about just one of the key geometric shapes. If you look, Sacred Geometry is the basis of nearly all Crystal Grid designs. They are not just to look symmetrical or appear mystical.

As already explained the crystalline structure of most minerals is geometric. The formations of certain crystals such as Quartz crystals show clear geometric shapes. These geometries form part of the synergistic power of Crystal Grids. The shapes and microscopic geometric patterns of crystals help form the energetic blueprint behind Crystal Grids.

Sacred Geometry is used to align with greater energies such as those of the Earth and the Universe. Crystals are arranged into these shapes to plug into these geometric energy fields and focus the energies of the crystals towards a desired result. Tapping into the Earth's energy field and Ley Lines helps manifest things in the Physical World, where they are needed.

By using Sacred Geometry you are also making sure that your desire or goal is in alignment with that of the Universe and the greater plan or purpose for your life.

Numerology

Numerology is the metaphysical science of numbers and their meaning. The belief in the spiritual significance of numbers is also ancient and can be found in many cultures, religions and traditions all around the world.

Although most people are more familiar with numerology being applied to names and birth dates for personality and destiny analysis, it has lots of other applications. The symbolic meaning of numbers has been used in Temples, religious, magical or shamanic ceremonies, dream interpretation and art.

Numerology is closely related and some would say the very root of Sacred Geometry. A single point in space becomes two, forming a line. Add another point to make three and we get the first geometric shape, the triangle. The symbolic meaning of numbers is very similar to that of their related geometric shapes. In a Crystal Grid we would use three crystals to form a triangle, so naturally the number three and the triangle both hold a very similar significance and power that you may want to tap into.

Manifesting

Manifesting is a metaphysical term used to describe the process of creating something in your life or the world. This could be drawing a situation, opportunity, new job or significant person into your life.

This is based on the belief that all humans have a spiritual creative power. That we can attract things into our life, if we focus on them. Everything around us is made of energy, including ourselves. So it makes sense that employing the right use and amount of energy could attract something or change things in our life. These energetic changes are believed to influence the Physical World around us, which is made of energy too.

There is now a lot of information, techniques and methods to manifest things out there. Crystal Grids are just one way. You will be programming or infusing your crystals and the grid with your desired intention. These energies are meant to alter the energy of a situation, open new doors to change or attract your wishes. Crystal Grids do go beyond the world of just manifesting our goals like creating better finances for example. They can be used to create a peaceful environment, bring healing or receive divine guidance for example. The possibilities are endless.

Your Intention

As with all aspects of Crystal Healing, I believe that your intention is what is going to really matter the most. Having a clear intention as to what it is you want to manifest or happen is essential. Really think about what it is that you want and why you want it. Be sure this is something that you would like to happen in your life and that you are prepared to really act on this, should it happen.

The Crystal Grids in this book are designed for different purposes, but see them as guides. They can always be personalised for your unique situation. Being clear about exactly what it is you wish to happen is going to really help you a lot.

Although it is also worth remembering not to be too specific that we limit ourselves. This can happen if we state exactly how we think the outcome will manifest. Watch that you are not too rigid or controlling that you actually block opportunities or something that is even better than you dreamed. You should try to avoid things like "I will get x amount of money by this time next month through the sale of my House". It would be better to say, "My Home will sell with ease".

I will give you a suggestion for the wording of your statement of intention for each of the grids, which you can use to base yourself on. You can use these as they are or adapt them for your specific needs. Always remember these are your words of power so keep them positive, clear and empowering.

I believe we are more like co-creators with the divine, manifesting is not as simple as some have made out. There are lots of factors involved and timing is not something that can be easily controlled by anyone. The important thing is to be clear about what you want but not too specific about 'how' exactly it will happen. Your crystal clear intention will program the Crystal Grid and make sure that it is in alignment with your goal.

The other thing that can take all your manifestation work to the next level is using visualisation. While you are programming your crystals with your intention, you want to really see it and feel it as if it were manifested already. Visualise your desired result and all the blessings that it brings to you and to others involved.

Charge this vision by feeling all the positive emotions like joy, satisfaction and peace you would feel if it were happening now. For something like healing, see the person in perfect health. For an end to arguments in the Home, see everyone getting along again and feel the good energy filling your House.

Your vision and emotions add power to your Crystal Grids. They imprint the energy with more clarity on how this could look and how you or others want to feel. This is not always conveyed in words. If you struggle with this part you may need to consider why you are creating the Crystal Grid. Make sure you are not manifesting something that you think you should have.

As with anything like this it is worth also remembering to make sure that your use of Crystal Grids is ethical. If you alter the purpose of a grid here or create your own, make sure that it is not in any way trying to control another person or cause harm. It is always best to ask someone for permission if you want to use a Crystal Grid to help them with things like protection or healing. Although you may mean well, you need to get permission. There may be valid exceptions, such as when a person is unable to communicate after an accident or illness for example.

This is a very personal thing that will vary from person to person. Only you can decide what is right for you. It's a good idea to add to your intention that the healing or protection be sent to someone only if it is for their highest good. This makes sure that you are not doing anything that you should not be doing or violating anyone's free will. I have inbuilt this into the intention statements for the Crystal Grids in this book for you.

A Complete & Balanced Approach

It's important to remember that no matter what you do on an energetic or spiritual level, you must also take physical action where possible. Crystal Grids can help you manifest your goals and make changes but should not be used as a substitute for the time and work needed to get to where you want to be. Crystal Grids are not a magic bullet for all your problems.

The Universe does not work like a microwave meal. Things may take time to manifest. Although we have all heard stories of people that asked for something to come into their lives and then it happened the next day, this is not normal. If you created a Crystal Grid for a better paid job but do not actually apply for any jobs, there is very little chance you will be offered one. This is because your actions do not align with your intentions.

When you take the armchair approach to manifestation, you are sending very mixed signals to the Universe. If you're not prepared to put any effort or energy into getting that job, then why should the Universe help you? How much do you really want it? If you want something to happen you need to do as much as you possibly can to make it happen. You want to take spiritual action through the Crystal Grid. Take mental and emotional action by staying focused and positive about your goal. Take physical action by doing what needs to be done to get to where you want to be.

The Crystal Grid Diamond

To summarise how Crystal Grids work take a look at the following diagram. This diamond shows the different facets of energy that are used to crystallise your intentions into reality. Crystal Healing, Sacred Geometry, Numerology, Intention and Action in the centre.

All these forces need to be working together. Without a clear intention or purposeful action, the diamond is broken and incomplete.

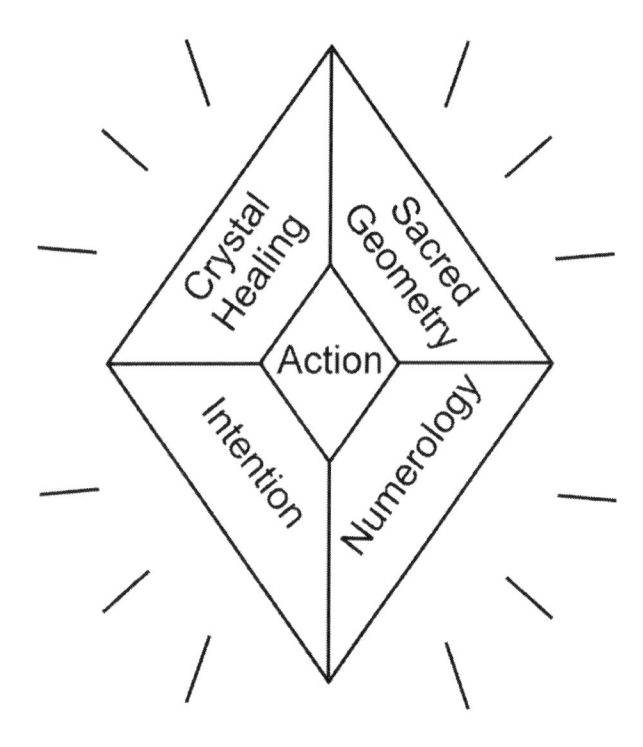

CRYSTAL GRIDS POWER

3

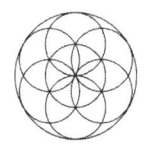

SACRED GEOMETRY REFERENCE GUIDE

This is an introduction and illustrated guide to the geometric shapes and symbols of Sacred Geometry that are used in the creation of most Crystal Grids you will find. These geometric shapes are the components of all the Crystal Grids featured in this book. There are many layers of meaning to these symbols and different sources may have different viewpoints. We will look at some of the history and symbolism behind these geometric shapes, so that you can understand their meanings better. All the shapes come with their numerical correspondence.

What you will also learn is how these symbols can be used within Crystal Grids for different purposes. I have condensed this into the form of keywords for ease of use and quick reference. These keywords will summarise the energy and very essence of each geometric shape for you.

I do not want to bury you under complex science or metaphysics. It is not essential to know this to use Sacred Geometry. For those of you who are interested in doing further research, please see the Bibliography at the end of this book.

This guide can be used to familiarise yourself with these recurring geometric shapes and their key meanings. You can use this to better understand the energetic blueprint and mechanics behind the Crystal Grids inside this book. You can use it to unlock the secrets of other Crystal Grids too. You could also use this as a guide to help you create your own Crystal Grids if you want to. There is more about this later.

You may wonder how using some of these symbols, which have multiple meanings does not produce an unwanted result. The key here is your intention. The same applies to crystals used in Crystal Healing. Your intention directs the energies most needed the way you need them at the time.

○

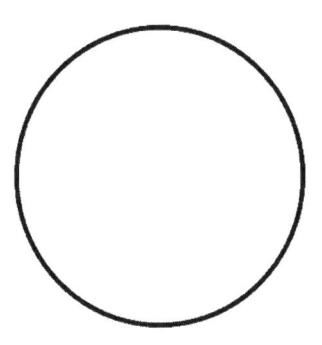

Circle

Keywords:

Protection, Wholeness, Renewal, Continuous Flow, Cosmic Support, Commitment, Focus, Unity

Numerical Vibration: 1, Infinity

History & Symbolism:

The Circle is believed to be the oldest symbol used by humans and has been used by all cultures in all ages. The Circle has no beginning or end, representing eternity. It can be drawn with one single line. Circular shapes can be seen in the celestial bodies of the Sun, Moon, Planets and the Earth. This ring shape is used as a sign of commitment in a wedding ring.

The Circle was also used to mark a clear boundary of protection to the ancients. This symbol is used in many protective amulets and talismans. Bracelets, beads and necklaces all use this continuous shape as a base. It can be seen in the Stone Circles at Sacred Sites in Europe and across the globe. You will find the Circle used for protection almost everywhere, even to this day.

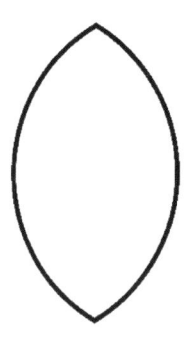

Vesica Piscis

Keywords:

Rebirth, Renewal, Creation, Creativity, Goddess, Transformation, New Opportunities, Spiritual Worlds

Numerical Vibration: 2

History & Symbolism:

This shape is also known as the *Mandorla,* which means almond in Latin. The word piscis like the astrological sign of Pisces comes from the Latin word for fish and it is the basis for the fish symbol used by Christianity. This shape can also be seen in medieval paintings surrounding Christian religious figures associated with rebirth and change. In nature it can be found in the petals of lotus flowers, leaves of plants and trees, lemons and the seeds of fruit.

The Vesica Piscis is formed by two converging circles, representing the Spiritual and Physical Worlds. It creates a shape which represents the feminine doorway to birth and new life. When we create something we need at least two forces or ingredients. The Vesica Piscis is a gateway to new experiences, new worlds and even other dimensions.

Spiral

Keywords:

Growth, Cosmic Support, Spiritual Development, Guidance, Focus, Wisdom, Kundalini Energy

Numerical Vibration: Infinity

History & Symbolism:

This is also one of the most ancient symbols. It can be found etched and painted onto cave walls and rocks all around the world. The Celts and the Maori revered this form. The Spiral shows a path of focused movement and intensified energy. In the natural world it can be seen in shells, ferns, Galaxies and even our DNA strands.

A Spiral can represent cosmic cycles of time, the Milky Way Galaxy and even the whole Universe. It can symbolise the coiled serpent like energy of the Kundalini, at the base of the spine or the Root Chakra. Snakes have been associated with knowledge and wisdom since ancient times. The Chakras themselves have been observed by some to look like a spiral of light.

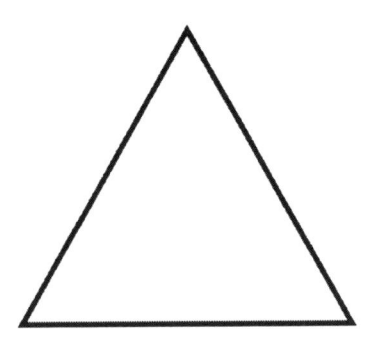

Triangle

Keywords:

Creativity, Creation, Manifestation, Harmony, Balance, Divine Connection, Intuition, Psychic Abilities, Inspiration, Raises Energy, Releases Energy, Protection

Numerical Vibration: 3

History & Symbolism:

This is one of the most mystical shapes. The Triangle is created by three lines and has three points, making it a representation of a trinity. This could be Mind, Body and Spirit, the Triple Goddess or the Holy Trinity. It is formed when two separate points create and are balanced by a third point.

It can be seen within the Sanskrit symbol for the Third Eye Chakra. When pointing up, a Triangle is a symbol of a flame and fire, or a torchlight that illuminates the darkness. It becomes a masculine symbol that raises energy upwards and connects with the divine. When reversed a Triangle becomes a cup that holds water or a vessel of spirit. It then becomes a feminine symbol, which anchors energy or receives spiritual information.

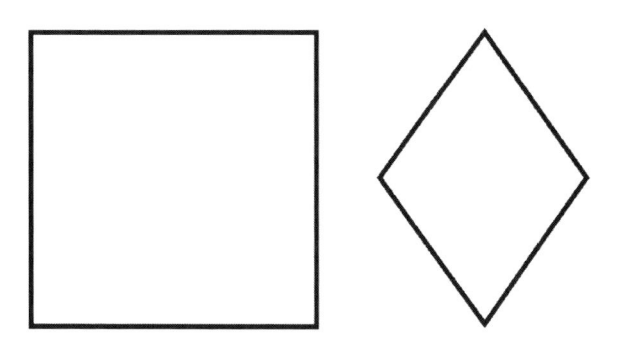

Square & Diamond

Keywords:

Stability, Strong Foundations, Strength, Endurance, Boundaries, Material Manifestation, The Four Directions, Seasons & Elements, Physical World, Environment, Grounding

Numerical Vibration: 4

History & Symbolism:

The Square is one of the strongest geometric shapes. It can be seen in some crystals like Pyrite and other natural rock formations. Think of it like a Castle or Fortress from above, or a brick that forms a House or a wall.

As the Diamond is one of the hardest stones it is also a symbol of strength and endurance. Both these four sided shapes represent the four directions of the compass, the four seasons and the four elements, fire, earth, water and air. The Square is also a symbol of the earth element itself and the Physical World.

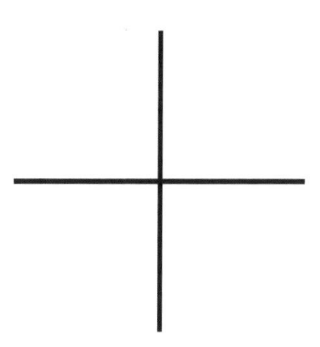

Cross

Keywords:

Protection, Physical & Spiritual Union, The Four Directions, Seasons & Elements, The Earth, The Solar Year, New Opportunities

Numerical Vibration: 4

History & Symbolism:

The Cross can be found the world over and in many forms. Two simple lines create four paths in four opposite directions. Like the Square it can represent the four elements, four seasons and the four directions of the compass. It can also mark out the two equinoxes and two solstices of the solar year. In some traditions a crossroads is considered a magical place between our world and the Spiritual World.

The horizontal line can symbolise the Earth and the Physical World. The vertical line is like a beam of divine light piercing the land. Together they form a shape that shows the Physical and Spiritual Worlds merging to become one. The cross has been used as a symbol of spiritual protection in several ancient cultures for thousands of years.

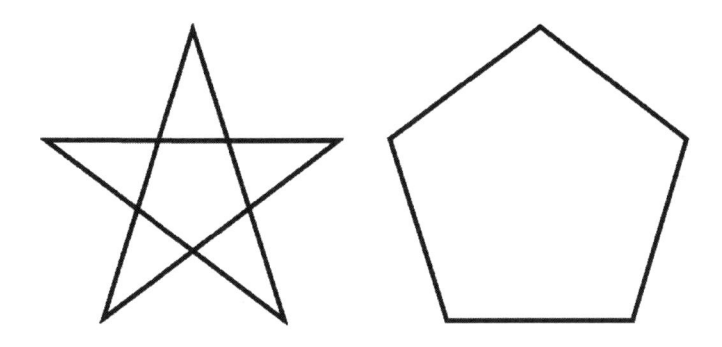

Pentagram & Pentagon

Keywords:

Rebirth, Renewal, Protection, Change, Freedom, New Beginnings, Four Elements & Spirit, Goddess

Numerical Vibration: 5

History & Symbolism:

Five pointed stars were used in Ancient Egypt to illustrate the stars in the night sky. The geometric form of the Pentagram was later used by Middle Eastern Mystics and Astrologers, long before it was brought to Europe. You can see pentagonal geometry in the petals of many flowers, the seeds in apples and even the human body.

The pentagram is associated with the movements of the Planet Venus and feminine Goddess energy. The five points can also represent the four elements with the fifth element of spirit. In numerology five alters the energy of the stable number four, creating movement and change. The forces of change are needed for creation and renewal of life.

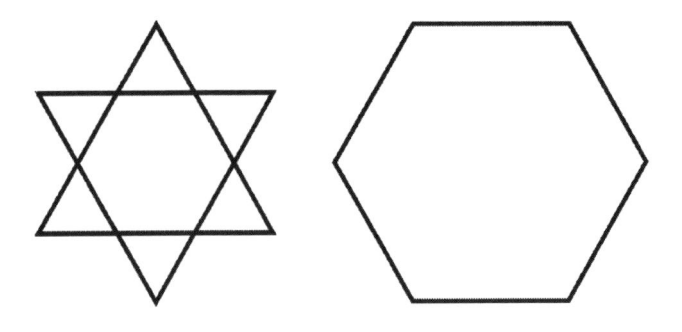

Star of David & Hexagon

Keywords:

Balance, Harmony, Cooperation, Partnerships, Protection, Spiritual Union, Divine Connection, Cosmic Alignment, Life Purpose, New Opportunities, Mastery, Lightbody Activation, Transmutation, Karmic Balance, Justice

Numerical Vibration: 6

History & Symbolism:

Also known as the *Shield of David*, *Seal of Solomon* or the *Hexagram*. Most know the Star of David as a Judaic symbol, associated with the Royal line of King David and King Solomon. This star symbol is also found in other cultures such as Tibet and India. Hexagonal geometry can be seen in many natural minerals and crystals, including Quartz. It can also be found in the structure of honeycomb.

The Star of David is formed by two interlinking Triangles. One pointing up and the other down, symbolising the union of opposites in perfect harmony. The symbol can also be used to create the four alchemical symbols of the elements. Combined together they become the star of the fifth element of spirit. The six pointed star has a long history as a powerful symbol of protection from evil.

Septagram & Septagon

Keywords:

Victory, Success, Wisdom, Knowledge, Study, Spirituality, Esoteric Knowledge, Elementals, Angelic Connection, Major Chakras

Numerical Vibration: 7

History & Symbolism:

The star shown with long points is also known as the *Elven Star* or the *Pleiadian Star*. The Septagram represents many sacred sevens from around the world. The seven classical Planets of Astrology, the seven Archangels, the seven stars of the Pleiades constellation, the seven days of the week, the seven Major Chakras and the seven metals of the Alchemists. This is where it gets its association with ancient knowledge and spiritual wisdom.

In the Kabbalah the seven pointed star is connected to the sphere of Netzach, which represents victory. In the Tarot, the seventh card is The Chariot, also associated with victory and success. Sphinxes sometimes appear on this card. In mythology the Sphinx is considered a guardian of secret knowledge. To many the Septagram is associated with elemental beings also known as nature spirits.

Octagram & Octagon

Keywords:

Prosperity, Abundance, Expansion, Growth, Progress, Success, Stability, Balance, Determination

Numerical Vibration: 8

History & Symbolism:

The Octagram can be formed by two overlapping Squares, which shows its strong connection to the Physical World. The eight points can represent the eight directions of the compass and the eight seasonal feast days of the Pagan wheel of the year.

The Octagram is also known as the *Star Of Lakshmi*, after the Hindu Goddess of wealth. Eight is seen as an auspicious number in many Asian Countries and in the practice of Feng Shui. The Octagram is used frequently in Islamic art and in the structure of holy buildings. In Buddhism eight is associated with the eightfold path of the Buddha, symbolised by a wheel with eight spokes.

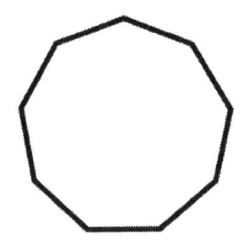

Enneagram & Enneagon

Keywords:

Completion, Achievement, Unity, Peace, Compassion, Humanity, Talents & Abilities

Numerical Vibration: 9

History & Symbolism:

The Enneagram and Enneagon are formed from nine points. Nine is the number of completion, being the last single digit number. It contains all nine digits used to create all other numbers with the addition of zero.

A similar shape is used in the Enneagram System to represent the nine personality types. It takes about nine months for a human baby to grow and be born. Three times three equals nine, making it a magic number for many people. In Hinduism nine is associated with the Lord Brahma, the creator God. This geometric shape can be seen as inclusive of many different energies together.

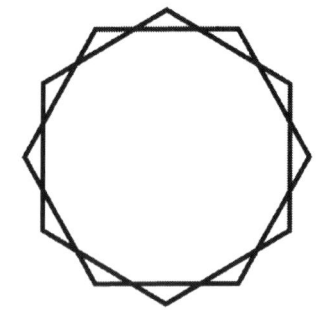

Dodecagram & Dodecagon

Keywords:

Celestial Connection, Astrological Alignment, The Zodiac, Perfection, The Universe, Life Purpose, Destiny, Twelve Chakra System, DNA Activation

Numerical Vibration: 12

History & Symbolism:

The twelve pointed Dodecagram can be formed by four interconnected triangles, two Stars of David or two hexagons. Historically it appears in an ancient Kabbalistic book about the order of creation as the *Sefer Yetzirah Symbol*. Twelve sided geometry corresponds to the twelve signs of the Western, Vedic and Chinese Zodiacs. In Western Astrology the twelve signs of the Zodiac are divided into four groups of three, which are ruled by the four elements. There are twelve months in the solar year.

The Dodecagram can be seen as a symbolic representation of the astrological and cosmic order of our Planet. Historically twelve turns up again and again as the twelve Knights of the Round Table, the Twelve Apostles and the twelve Tribes of Israel. In numerology twelve is seen as representing perfection.

Flower of Life

Keywords:

All Purpose, Balance, Harmony, Renewal, Manifestation, Creation, Creativity, The Universe

Numerical Vibration: 6, Infinity

History & Symbolism:

The Flower of Life is a symbol of mysterious origins. It is found all over the world from Ancient Egypt, India to Japan. It continues to be found in new places all the time. It is formed by 19 interlocking circles, which create overlapping flowers of Vesica Piscis shapes. Many if not all symbols of Sacred Geometry and even whole alphabets can be found embedded into its structure.

The hexagonal geometries of the Flower of Life can be seen in the formation of crystals like Quartz, Rubies, Emeralds and Sapphires for example. It is also seen hidden in nature inside fruit, flowers, cells and snowflakes. The Flower of Life has been described as holding the blueprint for the entire Universe.

Seed of Life

Keywords:

Creation, Creativity, Development, Growth, New Beginnings

Numerical Vibration: 7

History & Symbolism:

The Seed of Life can be found at the centre of the Flower of Life symbol. This flower like shape is created by seven overlapping circles, sometimes also enclosed by an eighth as shown here. Like its mother symbol the Flower of Life, these geometries can be seen in crystals, flowers and fruit. The Seed of Life symbol has been found in many places including Ancient Egyptian Temples, Medieval English Churches, Leonardo Da Vinci's sketches and the tombstone of a Templar Knight.

The Seed of Life is associated with the seven days of creation and the seven days of the week. Due to it being a component of the Flower of Life, the Seed of Life represents more the beginning of a creative cycle. It is the seed of the flower, holding in it the potential and energy to reach full bloom.

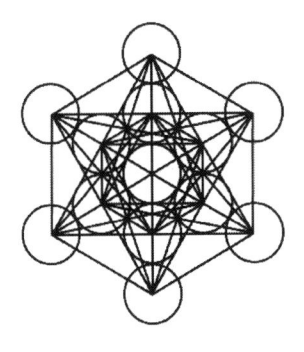

Metatron's Cube

Keywords:

Purification, Protection, Esoteric Knowledge, Wisdom, Spirituality, Angelic Connection, Akashic Records

Numerical Vibration: 6, 13

History & Symbolism:

This is another symbol of Sacred Geometry that contains within it many spiritually significant geometric shapes. This includes the Star of David, the Circle, the Merkaba and the cube. Metatron's Cube is often represented in three dimensional form but as a two dimensional symbol as shown here, it contains thirteen circles.

This complex geometric shape is named after the Archangel Metatron. This is a powerful angel who is said to record all history within a sacred book. Archangel Metatron is associated with divine knowledge and wisdom. The five Platonic Solids can be found within this multidimensional symbol. Many of the geometric shapes that make up Metratron's Cube are considered powerful symbols of protection around the world.

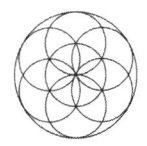

4

CRYSTAL GRID TOOLS & ESSENTIALS

When you begin working with Crystal Grids, you are going to start to notice that certain crystals are used quite often. Once you invest in a few of these crystal allies and tools, you can use them over and over again.

It is very helpful to understand how and why different types of crystals are used in certain positions. This will help you selecting the right form or cut of crystal. These rules are pretty simple and easy to remember, as the crystals used in Crystal Grids tend to fall into three main categories. These are the Central Stone, the Support Stones and an Activation Wand. See the illustration on the following page for an example of two of these.

All these crystals will mostly consist of polished Tumble Stones and natural or cut and polished Crystal Points. We will explore all these types of crystal forms in more detail in this chapter.

Central Stone

Support Stones

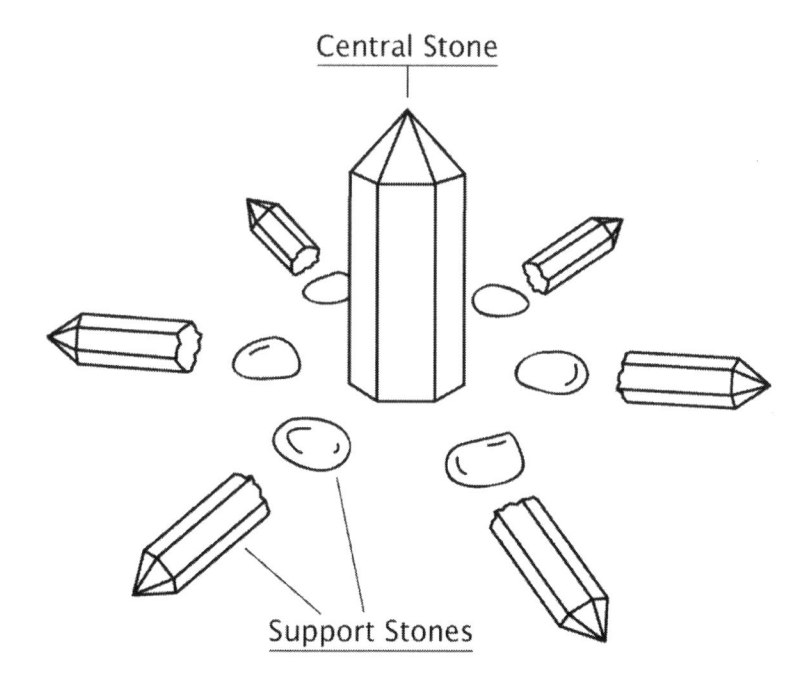

Central Stones

Nearly all the Crystal Grids featured in this book and pretty much all the ones you will find elsewhere, have some kind of Central Stone. This is the crystal that is at the very centre of the grid. This crystal is important as it represents the very heart of the grid's purpose.

The Central Stone is like the hub and power source for the entire arrangement of crystals. Its job is to hold the blueprint of the entire Crystal Grid and its intention. It transmits energy through all the other crystals and out into the Universe. The Central Stone also acts like an anchor point for the energies of the Crystal Grid and your intention.

With Body Crystal Grids there is rarely any need for a Central Stone. Your body and Aura are like the focal point of the grid. Other crystals may sometimes be placed on one or more Chakras to direct the energies there. With Location Crystal Grids sometimes a Central Stone is used but not always. These Crystal Grids often focus on the boundaries of a space, so crystals are usually placed around the outer edges of an area.

With Regular Crystal Grids the Central Stone should always be the largest crystal in the grid. The Central Stone should clearly look like the focal point of the entire arrangement of crystals. When selecting crystals remember to keep this in mind. What is good to know is that some Central Stones can be used for any Crystal Grid. I will get to this shortly. There are certain natural crystal formations and cut crystals, which make the best Central Stones in my experience. These forms work really well in the heart of your Crystal Grid and distribute the energy evenly. They can also enhance or multiply the energy of all the other crystals.

Recommended Central Stones

Here is my list of powerful and effective crystal forms for Central Stones. Don't worry if some of these sound unfamiliar to you, I will explain what these are later in this chapter.

Standing Crystal Point

Standing Generator Point

Crystal Pyramid

Crystal Sphere

Star of David Crystal

Crystal Flame

Crystal Skull

Crystal Heart

Crystal Merkaba

Support Stones

These are any crystal used in the layout of the Crystal Grid that is not the Central Stone. These crystals can be any shape, natural or polished, free standing or laying flat. They will tend to be part of a group of similar shaped crystals of the same type of stone.

There can be one or more sets of Support Stones used in a Crystal Grid. When this happens in this book, crystals surrounding the Central Stone in the inner part of a grid will be called Inner Support Stones. Any crystals that are on the outer edge of the grid will be called Outer Support Stones. The role of all Support Stones is to support the Crystal Grid and the Central Stone with their additional energies. They distribute these energies throughout the whole grid. You could see these crystals as being like the parts of the circuit board of a Crystal Grid.

The most commonly used types of Support Stones are Tumble Stones and Crystal Points. Support Stones in the form of Crystal Points, pointing outwards from the edge of the grid help send the energies and our intentions out into the Universe and world around us.

Activation Wand

This is a Crystal Wand you can use to activate your Crystal Grid. A Crystal Wand sounds a bit Harry Potter but it is really just a large and long Crystal Point. This could be a natural Crystal Point or a cut and polished Crystal Wand. There is a lot of choice for Crystal Wands you could use as an Activation Wand. You want something with faceted sides and a pointed termination point. Avoid what are sometimes called Massage Wands, which are smooth with no edges and have rounded tips. These lack the laser like focus of other Crystal Wands.

For the purpose of activating Crystal Grids use Clear Quartz rather than any other stone. By clear I just mean that a good part of the crystal is clear, it does not need to be perfect. If you are selecting an Activation Wand from crystals you already have or in a shop, hold them to see how they feel. A good Activation Wand should feel good in your hands and have a strong energy. If you're choosing one online then go with your intuition. You should be drawn to the right one for you.

Crystal Wands like any form of Crystal Point are used to direct and focus energies. You only need one of these crystals, which you can use for all your Crystal Grid work. An Activation Wand is used to program and activate the Crystal Grid.

This tool is not completely essential because I am going to show you three different methods to activate your Crystal Grids. Two use an Activation Wand but one does not. This is personal preference. You may want to wait before deciding if you want to invest in a Crystal Wand, if you don't already have one.

Tumble Stones

Also known as a Tumbled Stone. These are the easiest crystals to find and the most inexpensive form of crystal. They are ideal for placing around the Central Stone as Support Stones and bring in the properties of the mineral they are made from.

They are just pieces of crystal which have been tumble polished. Because of their freeform shape these crystals are not as good for directing energies. Tumble Stones send their energies in all directions. They can also have their energy directed by their geometric position within the Crystal Grid or by a nearby Crystal Point. If a Tumble Stone has an angular or cylinder shape they may be used in a similar way to Crystal Points.

If you are working with a very simple Crystal Grid, you could even use a Tumble Stone as the Central Stone. You should try to make sure that it is bigger than any other crystals used. You can get extra large Tumble Stones. For the best results try one of the recommended forms of Central Stones listed earlier.

Crystal Points

These are really useful crystals to have and can be used to form the geometric patterns around the Central Stone. These smaller Crystal Points are usually laid flat on the grid but could also be free Standing Crystal Points. Clear Quartz, Citrine, Smoky Quartz and Amethyst crystals all naturally grow as Crystal Points and are easily available.

The benefit of these crystal formations is that they direct and focus energies at the tip, also known as the termination point. By creating channels for energy to pass through and out of them, they are ideal crystals for Crystal Grids. They work well within the geometric lines that make up the grids.

You can get stones that have been cut and polished into these shapes, which will also work just as well. Natural or cut Crystal Points will cost you more than Tumble Stones. It is worth mentioning that with natural raw Crystal Points, you will see many flaws and they may not look perfect. This does not weaken their effectiveness for directing the flow of energy throughout the Crystal Grid.

A Guide To Different Crystal Forms

In this section I will describe the main uses of different crystal cuts, carvings and natural formations as they are used within Crystal Grids. Understanding the way different forms of crystals work will really help you in selecting crystals to use in your grids. It is also valuable knowledge to have with any work you do with crystals or Crystal Healing.

I have also given a few suggestions for the types of Crystal Grid that some of these forms are well suited to. To make things easier, especially if you are new to crystals, I have included some illustrations of these different shapes and forms. Please refer to the following diagram for a general guide to the way these crystal forms look to help you identify them.

CRYSTAL GRIDS POWER

Crystal Shapes & Forms

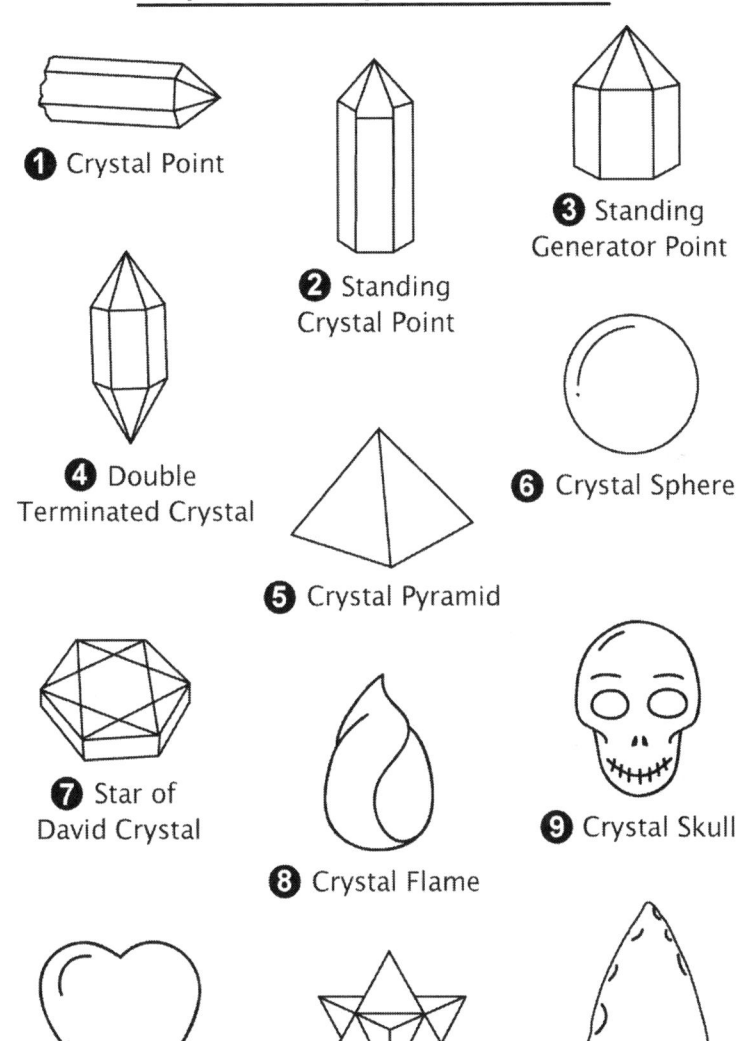

❶ Crystal Point

❷ Standing Crystal Point

❸ Standing Generator Point

❹ Double Terminated Crystal

❺ Crystal Pyramid

❻ Crystal Sphere

❼ Star of David Crystal

❽ Crystal Flame

❾ Crystal Skull

❿ Crystal Heart

⓫ Crystal Merkaba

⓬ Crystal Arrowhead

(1) Crystal Point

This is a natural or cut crystal with a single tip or termination point at one end. If selecting Quartz Crystal Points for Crystal Grids look for a good amount of clarity. These crystals direct and focus energies out the termination point. The base or root of the crystal can also be used to absorb and draw off energies.

(2) Standing Crystal Point

This is a natural or cut Crystal Point, which either naturally stands pointing up or has been cut at the base. These freestanding crystals are sometimes called Towers. They focus and beam energy upwards, making them ideal Central Stones. They can also be used as Support Stones to increase energy.

(3) Standing Generator Point

A Generator Point is a natural or cut crystal that has six equally sized triangular faces around the tip or termination point. The termination point when viewed from above must also be in the centre of the crystal. Cut Crystal Points often use this shape. Generator Points build up and transmit energies, which makes them excellent Central Stones.

(4) Double Terminated Crystal

This is a natural or cut Crystal Point with a termination point at both ends. These special crystals send and receive energies at the same time. They can also be used to transmute energies. Double Terminated Crystals are good Support Stones for connecting two other crystals within a Crystal Grid.

(5) Crystal Pyramid

These cut and polished stones are usually four sided with a flat base. They anchor, raise and focus energy out through the tip, making them a good choice for a Central Stone. Small Crystal Pyramids could also be used anywhere in the grid. They work well in cross and square shaped grids. You can use pyramids in any Crystal Grid for raising or amplifying energies. They work well in grids for manifesting things or balancing Earth energies.

(6) Crystal Sphere

Also known as a Crystal Ball. This is a stone that has been cut and polished into a perfect sphere. You will need a stand to keep them in place within the grid. Some stands will come supplied with Crystal Spheres. This cut focuses and directs energies in all directions evenly, making them good Central Stones. They work well in Grids for focus, awakening psychic abilities or for peace and harmony.

(7) Star of David Crystal

This is a cut and polished crystal with many facets. The overall shape is hexagonal with the facets forming a Star of David geometric shape. These are not so easy to find but they make great Central Stones. Due to the geometries they connect and direct energies in many directions within a Crystal Grid. They work well in hexagonal Crystal Grids. They are good in grids for protection, balance, unity or life purpose.

(8) Crystal Flame

This is a crystal that has been carved into a flame like shape. They will have a flat base and gently twisting or spiraling formation. Crystal Flames are not common but can be used as Central Stones. They generate and focus energies while directing them upwards. Fire element energies are also helpful for transmuting energies. Crystal Flames are good for Crystal Grids focused on cleansing, gaining knowledge or boosting energy.

(9) Crystal Skull

This is a crystal that has been carved into a skull shape. They can be expensive but smaller ones are more affordable. Crystal Skulls bring in the help of spiritual beings such as your guides or ancestors. They are also known for being powerful healing stones. Another good Central Stone especially for guidance, knowledge, protection and healing grids.

(10) Crystal Heart

This is any crystal that has been carved into the shape of a heart. They radiate energies in all directions. They can be used as either a Central Stone or smaller Support Stones. This form would suit any Crystal Grid focused on love, relationships, peace or health and healing.

(11) Crystal Merkaba

This is a crystal that has been cut into a mystical geometric shape also known as a Merkaba Star or Merkabah. In geometry it is also known as a Star Tetrahedron. Crystal Merkabas have eight points to direct and focus their energies in many different directions. They are used in Crystal Grids for spiritual development, raising the vibration, affecting the Aura, personal transformation and protection.

(12) Crystal Arrowhead

Making Arrowheads from stone is an ancient tradition going back to prehistoric times. They are still made by hand today, by chipping away at Obsidian. Although other stones can be cut this way, the most easily available are Obsidian. Obsidian Arrowheads direct energies out the tip and can be used for strong psychic protection. Crystal Arrowheads can also be used to sever the connection with a person or energy that is harmful. They also tap into your inner warrior. They are good stones for Crystal Grids for protection, releasing things, inner strength or life direction.

Recommended Crystals for Grids

Clear Quartz is perfect for any kind of Crystal Grid. This crystal is a powerful tool for manifestation work or healing. Clear Quartz is highly programmable, meaning that it retains your intentions. This crystal sends and receives energy really well. Clear Quartz brings focus, clarity and power to all your Crystal Grids. The following two forms of this crystal will prove very wise investments to have for all Crystal Grids.

Clear Quartz Crystal Points

You want to have a set of 6, 8 or ideally 12 Clear Quartz Crystal Points. Try to look for crystals that are roughly about the same size, but no smaller than one and a half inches in length. You can also use Double Terminated Crystal Points. These crystals will direct, connect and enhance the energy of other crystals in the grid. They will be used in many of the Crystal Grids featured in this book, so they will be very useful crystals to have.

Clear Quartz Standing Crystal Point

This crystal can be used for any Crystal Grid in this book that requires a Central Stone. The Crystal Point will beam your intentions out into the Universe with clarity. It will build a strong energy to power your Crystal Grids. This will also amplify and focus the energy of all other crystals in the grid. You can substitute one of these crystals if my suggested Central Stone is not available.

Notepaper

I like to use notes in my Crystal Grids. You can write a brief summary of your intention on a small piece of paper. Then fold it up and place it under the Central Stone. This further confirms your intention in physical form. It also helps set and focus of the Crystal Grid after it has been activated. I include a suggested statement of intention with each grid in this book, which you can use as a guide to creating a written affirmation.

Many people feel it helps to write down their goals and intentions. It has been found that people who write down their goals have a higher success rate than those that don't. What better way to do this than placing your written intention at the centre of your Crystal Grid? You can use any paper you like, notepaper, parchment paper or coloured paper. Avoid anything with printed words or images that are not in alignment with the intention of your Crystal Grid. As the note will be part of your Crystal Grid, you should cleanse it along with all the crystals and include it with them when you activate the grid.

Photographs

Just like the addition of a note with your Crystal Grid, a photograph can be used to represent the person a grid has been made for. This is common practice with distant healing or distant protection grids. Just like writing their name on paper, the photo will help create a stronger connection between the grid and the person it has been made for. This is not needed when you're doing a Crystal Grid only for yourself.

Try to avoid photos with extra people in, unless your grid is for all those people shown. Use a recent portrait photo or whole body photo with no other people showing. If printing out photos yourself, it is easy to crop other people out of the photo. Of course if your grid is aimed at helping a couple or your family then this would not be an issue. If the Crystal Grid is for healing or spiritual purposes you could even use an Aura photo if they have a recent one.

All photos used should be cleansed and included in the activation method. Place the photo face up under the Central Stone along with your note of intention. I will let you know when a photo is helpful for a particular grid. This is always optional and if no photo is available, you can just use their name on notepaper as described above.

Maps

In some Crystal Grids you could also include a small map. This would be for grids that are used to send healing or bring peace to a specific location for example. This may be a Town, City, Country, Island or even an Ocean. You can print maps from the Internet easily. These are folded with the notepaper and placed under the Central Stone. This is also optional, you can just mention the location in the affirmation of intention note.

Crystal Grid Templates

This is not essential but many people do find that using some kind of physical layout for their Crystal Grids to be helpful. This can consist of a piece printed or hand drawn paper or card. With the growing interest in Crystal Grids you can now get geometric designs printed onto Crystal Grid Cloths. There are some that have been etched onto metal, such as copper or brass. You can also get Crystal Grid Templates that are engraved onto wooden discs or squares that you can use as a base.

The benefit of Crystal Grid Templates like these is that they make it easier to position the crystals. If you need to clean the crystals or they are knocked out of place, you can see where they belong straight away. You really don't need to invest in these items unless you want to. Later on I am going to give you a printable PDF file with all the Crystal Grid Templates from this book.

If you don't have access to a printer, do not worry because you don't need to use a template to create Crystal Grids. Some people prefer to place their grids directly onto a flat surface. If you work this way, you can make your grids as big or as small as you like. All the grids in this book come with clear diagrams, which you can use as a guide to crystal placement. Crystal Grids do not need to be absolutely perfect to work.

If a Crystal Grid uses the Flower of Life symbol, you may want to invest in a Crystal Grid Cloth for these. This will be very useful to you and inexpensive if you can't print the Flower of Life out yourself. You can purchase these online.

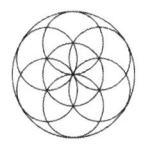

5

HOW TO PREPARE YOUR CRYSTAL GRID

Before you begin arranging your crystals into their positions, there are a few things that need to be done in preparation. If you are familiar with Crystal Healing, some of these procedures will be very familiar to you and you may want to skip forward to the Crystal Grid Activation Methods later in this chapter.

Each time you create a new Crystal Grid, you will want to start with crystals that have been cleansed. Any new crystals could also be consecrated which I will explain. This is optional but a good idea.

You will then have to decide if you want to use the Activation Wand method, the simpler All-In-One method or a combination of the two. All of these methods will work as long as you feel comfortable using them. The Activation Wand method is the most well known, but some people find it a bit complicated. See how you feel when you read about them.

You will not have chosen a Crystal Grid to use yet but I want you to understand the procedure and familiarise yourself before you start making any grids from this book. When you're ready to start setting up a Crystal Grid, you can return to this chapter and follow the steps below.

Cleansing Your Crystals

You must use crystals that have been energetically cleansed and rebalanced for the creation of Crystal Grids. By cleansing I mean clear any energies they may have picked up while in a shop, from any previous owners, through their travels, from you or from past use. You don't want any previous energies or intentions to cloud or confuse your intention once your Crystal Grid is set up and activated.

There are many ways to cleanse or purify your crystals. If you are already familiar with cleansing crystals and have your own ways of doing this, then keep doing what works for you. Here are some possible options. I do not personally recommend using water, direct sunlight or salt to cleanse crystals as these can damage some minerals. Also all the methods below do not require waiting for special times such as the Full Moon, just to make things easier for you. Always use what feels right and works for you.

Cleansing Crystals With Incense

You can smudge them with the smoke of a bundle of dry White Sage, also known as a Smudge Stick. You can also cleanse them by passing them through the fragrant smoke of a stick of Palo Santo wood. Or use cleansing incense like Sandalwood, Sage, Copal, Camphor, Frankincense and Myrrh or any purifying incense blend.

Always use a fireproof dish or an incense holder. Light the incense stick or wood and blow out the flame, so that it smoulders. Pass the crystals through the smoke with the intention to cleanse them three times or until you feel that they are clear.

Cleansing Crystals With Sacred Sound

You can also cleanse crystals using sacred sound. You can use a Tibetan Singing Bowl by placing your crystals around it but not inside the bowl. Firmly strike the side of the metal bowl with the wooden mallet and then rub the side in a circular clockwise motion with the mallet to maintain the ringing sound. The crystals should be all clear after about a minute of this.

A simpler method is to use Tibetan Ting Shas. These are small brass cymbals with Buddhist mantras or designs. Place your crystals in front of you on a flat surface. Hold the Ting Shas by the rope that connects them, so that they are dangling down next to each other over your crystals. Bring the sides of the cymbals together firmly so they ring and let this fade away. Then repeat two more times. Your crystals are now clear.

Cleansing Crystals With Pyramid Power

If you work with crystals a lot, this could be a useful investment. Copper Pyramids, made from copper bars or pipes can be used to cleanse crystals. They should be made to the proportions of the Great Pyramid at Giza. Align one of the sides of the Copper Pyramid to magnetic North using a compass. Now all you need to do is place your crystals inside and under the middle of the Copper Pyramid. Your crystals should be cleansed and rebalanced within an hour or leave them overnight.

Cleansing Crystals With Energy

If you use any type of energy healing modality, you may already use this for cleansing items like crystals. This may be Reiki, Seichim or any other healing system. Usually this will involve holding the crystals with both hands, while sending the healing energy through the hands into the crystals. These methods may require special training, initiation or an attunement.

If you are new to cleansing crystals, one of the quickest and easiest ways is using Universal White Light. This method uses a simple visualisation that anyone can do. You are going to use the purifying power of white light energy. With this method no other special tools or skills are needed, just your mind's eye and intention. If you are cleansing a lot of crystals and can't hold them all in your hands all at once, just repeat the procedure for different batches of crystals.

How To Cleanse Your Crystals With Universal White Light

1. Find a quiet place where you will not be disturbed. Sit down with your legs crossed if you can or use a chair. Close your eyes and take three deep breaths.

2. Hold your crystals in your hands. One hand over the other if possible or cupped.

3. Now visualise a beam of pure white light coming down from above into your Crown Chakra (At the top of your head) down to the Heart Chakra (the centre of your chest). Moving out along your arms and into your hands.

4. See this Universal White Light in your mind's eye filling the crystals and surrounding them.

5. Focus on clearing them as you say out loud or in your head *"I cleanse, purify and rebalance these crystals of all negative, unbalanced or fear based energies, now!"*

6. Wait a few moments or when you feel this has been done, open your eyes. You may need to take some time before you get up again.

Consecrating New Crystals

It is a good idea to consecrate any new crystals. This is also called dedicating or blessing and is related to programming. Consecrating is really just setting your intention, so that the crystal always works for the highest good. It also adds some protection to your crystals.

As you are using crystals to bring about changes, which may affect others, you want to make sure there is no chance you can interfere with things or make a situation worse. This is unlikely but safeguards this from ever happening. Also if you were to use them in a way that was not entirely ethical even with good intentions, the crystal would have little or no effect.

Programming is really just a way to direct and use the energy of a crystal for a very specific task or purpose. Consecrating crystals to only serve the highest good is a bit like installing the operating system on your computer. It is the default behavior of your crystals regardless of how you use them in the future.

You only need to do this once before you first use your new crystals. You always want to consecrate new crystals after they have been cleansed for the very first time. Once consecrated you never have to consecrate them again. Cleansing them in the future will not erase the consecration.

If you already have crystals that you have used but feel you would like to consecrate them, you can do so. You are going to be connecting with divine energy, this is a very personal thing so I have offered some alternative words you could use if you are not comfortable or familiar with the words "Creator Source". Feel free to also add to this any spiritual Guides, Deities, Angels or Ascended Masters that you work with.

How To Consecrate Your Crystals

1. Find a quiet place where you will not be disturbed. Sit down with your legs crossed if you can or sit on a chair. Take three deep breaths before you begin.

2. Hold your Crystals using both hands in front of you, just above eye level (This is the position of the Third Eye Chakra).

3. Say out loud or to yourself *"I dedicate these crystals to the Creator Source (Or God, Goddess, Great Spirit, Divine Light, Universe, Infinite Intelligence, Source Energy, All-That-Is etc.) Please bless and protect these crystals. May these crystals serve and only serve my highest and greatest good and the highest and greatest good of all"*

Once you have cleansed and possibly consecrated all your crystals they are ready to be put in place and activated. There are three activation methods below and you only need to select one of these.

1. The Activation Wand Method

This is the most well known method for activating a Regular Crystal Grid. It requires the use of a large Crystal Point or cut and polished Crystal Wand. As explained earlier in the chapter on tools, you want to use Clear Quartz for this job.

Your Activation Wand should be cleansed and consecrated before use, just like your other crystals. You can do this all at the same time to make things easier. You are going to be using the Activation Wand to program all the crystals in your grid. All this really means is that the wand acts as a tool to transfer your intention for the Crystal Grid to all the crystals.

Crystals naturally record and store energies and information. Programming a crystal is simply communicating to the crystal what you want help with so they can help you. You could call this process charging the crystal with your intention. The Mineral Kingdom is happy to help us. Throughout this book I will be using the word program for this process. As an alternative, when you activate your grids you could say something like "*I charge this crystal grid with my intention to...*" or an even more personal approach "*I ask these crystals to assist me with...*"

Activating your Crystal Grid also connects the crystals to the Central Stone and with each other. Once completed the grid is activated, meaning it is now working and broadcasting your intentions. I just want to make it clear that there is no one right way to set up and activate a Crystal Grid. This popular method can seem complicated to some and those new to Crystal Grids.

Do not worry too much about whether you are doing it right. In the beginning it may feel like you are having to remember the procedure and it may not feel very natural to you. Like anything over time this will fade away and you may even develop your own personal ways to activate your grids. This is just a way for you to get started. This is also why I am also including the simpler method in this book that does not use a Crystal Wand at all.

How To Activate a Crystal Grid With an Activation Wand

1. Arrange all your crystals and anything else needed into position before you start. Start with the Central Stone and work outwards.

2. Sit for a few moments holding your Activation Wand in your hands with eyes closed. Take three deep breaths and get really clear about your intention.

3. Open your eyes. Hold the Activation Wand with both hands. Point the tip of the Activation Wand towards the top of the Central Stone. It may help to visualise a beam of light leaving your Activation Wand and entering the Central Stone.

4. Focus on your desired result, use visualisation and emotion. See it and feel it as manifested now. Say to yourself or out loud a statement of your Crystal Grid's intention. You can use the one I have included with all Crystal Grids in this book or create your own: *"I program this Crystal Grid for..."* or *"I charge this Crystal Grid to..."* or *"I ask these crystals to assist me with..."*

5. Still focusing on your intention trace a line with the Activation Wand from the Central Stone to one of the Support Stones from the inner part of the grid, then return back to the Central Stone (See the following diagram). It may help to start from the Support Stone at the top, 12 o'clock position. If only one set of Support Stones is used then go to those. Repeat for each of the crystals in that group, going around clockwise. You could visualise the beam of light joining up the crystals like the spokes of a wheel.

6. Now point the Activation Wand at this group or ring of Support Stones and join them up to each other. Trace a circle or square depending on the design of the Crystal Grid. Go around in a clockwise direction until you get back to the first crystal (See the following diagram).

Start from the Support Stone at the top or 12 o'clock position. Connecting Support Stones in a circular way will work for all shapes but if you prefer you can also trace the geometric pattern, such as the star design. If Crystal Points or Arrowheads are used that point anticlockwise, you would go that way instead for these.

7. Now repeat steps 5 and 6 for the Outer Support Stones in the grid if there are more. Connecting each crystal to the Central Stone. Then connecting each Support Stone in the group with each other as before.

Activation Wand Directions

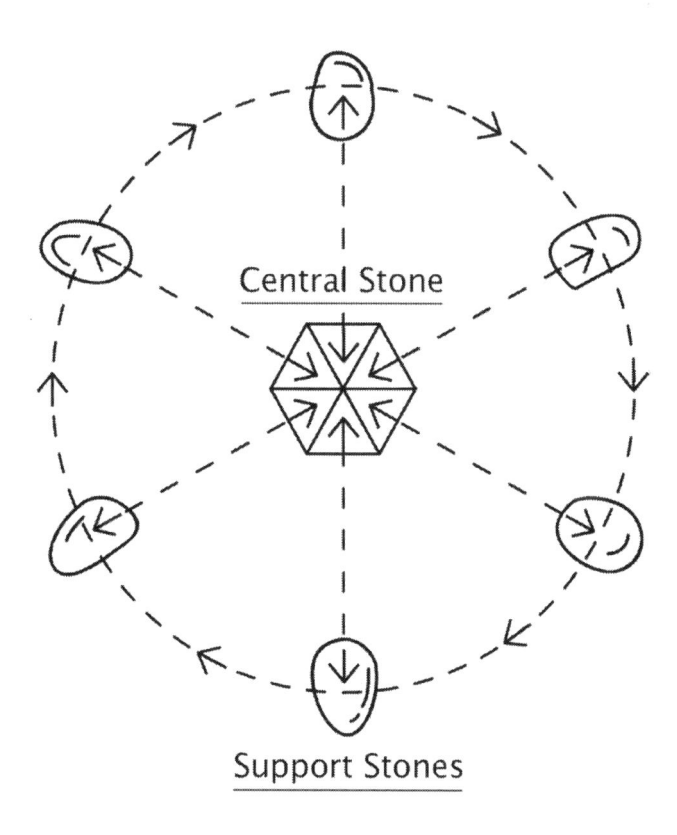

Central Stone

Support Stones

2. The All-In-One Method

This programming based All-In-One method of Crystal Grid activation is much more simple. It is also ideal for activating Location Crystal Grids and Body Crystal Grid layouts. No Activation Wand, extra crystals or tools are needed. The method is quicker and less complex. With not so much to think about, some may find this easier to work with, but it really is up to you. Both methods will work.

The crystals are not joined by the activation crystal but by your intention. They are activated once they have all been laid out in their geometric pattern. This method of activation is the same as you would use to program a crystal. You are just instructing the crystals with your desired intention for the Crystal Grid. This is transferred from you directly to the crystals, without the use of an Activation Wand.

How To Activate a Crystal Grid All-In-One

1. Hold all your crystals in your hands if possible. If not work in batches.

2. Sit for a few moments with your eyes closed. Take three deep breaths and get really clear about your intention.

3. Raise your crystals up in front of your Third Eye Chakra. Between and just above your eyes.

4. Focus on your desired result, use visualisation and emotion. See it and feel it as manifested now. Say to yourself or out loud a statement of your Crystal Grid's intention. You can use the one I have included with all Crystal Grids in this book or create your own: *"I program this Crystal Grid for..."* or *"I charge this*

Crystal Grid to..." or *"I ask these crystals to assist me with..."*

5. Lastly arrange your crystals into position to form your Crystal Grid. Start with the Central Stone (If it has one) and then work outwards.

3. The Combination Method

This is a method I have created that combines elements of both methods but still in a simplified form. If you are still drawn to working with an Activation Wand but find the activation wand method a bit too much, then this may suit you better. You will be using a Crystal Wand to program the entire grid through the Central Stone, so it is only suitable for Regular Crystal Grids.

How To Activate a Crystal Grid with the Combination Method

1. Arrange all your crystals and anything else needed into position before you start. Start with the Central Stone and work outwards.

2. Sit for a few moments holding your Activation Wand in your hands with eyes closed. Take three deep breaths and get really clear about your intention.

3. Open your eyes. Hold the Activation Wand using both hands. Point the tip of the Activation Wand towards the top of your Central Stone. It may help to visualise a beam of light leaving your Activation Wand and entering the Central Stone.

4. Focus on your desired result, use visualisation and emotion. See it and feel it as manifested now. Say to yourself or out loud a statement of your Crystal Grid's intention. You can use the one I have included with all Crystal Grids in this book or create your own: *"I program this Crystal Grid for..."* or *"I charge this Crystal Grid to..."* or *"I ask these crystals to assist me with..."*

Crystal Grid Placement Considerations

Always place your Crystal Grids on a flat surface where they will not be easily disturbed. Give your Crystal Grid some breathing space, even from nearby crystals or any other grids. Avoid areas that are also dumping grounds for other items such as keys, phones, letters, bills, junk mail, magazines or drinks.

You are creating a sacred space here. Other nearby items may not only knock the crystals in your grid but they also disturb the energy very easily. You do not want to place a Crystal Grid right next to the TV or a computer for this reason. I would also avoid placing a Crystal Grid on a bedside cabinet. This will almost certainly get knocked. A Crystal Grid is very energising and will likely disturb your sleep. The crystals may also absorb too many of your thoughts from dreams. The exception would be sleep or dream related grids.

Pets and children may also pose a problem but this is hard to avoid. If you can select places that are a little higher or out of the way it may help. If you see crystals have been moved, just put them back as soon as possible. The tops of chests of drawers, cabinets, sideboards, small tables, window sills and Home altars are all a good choice. Some people like to align their grids with magnetic North. Explain to others you live with that you have placed it there and that you do not want them to touch or move it and they should understand.

Feng Shui Placement Ideas

I do not think it is essential that you use Feng Shui or place your Crystal Grid in a specific room in the Home. This may be something that you wish to experiment with later as you work more with Crystal Grids. Test things out and see if following these systems is helpful for your grids and brings better or faster results for you.

The subject of Feng Shui is vast and way beyond the scope of this book. How you would use Feng Shui with Crystal Grids is up to you. A good idea would be to place the grid in the part of the Home that relates to the purpose of the grid. In traditional Feng Shui, which goes back thousands of years, a compass is used. This helps determine the different sectors of a building as they relate to the magnetic field of the Earth and the elements. These sectors represent different life areas like career, relationships or wealth.

So a Crystal Grid for abundance would work well in the Wealth Sector of the Home. A Crystal Grid for healing could be placed in the Health Sector. This is not always easy as you do not want to put a Crystal Grid in the bathroom, kitchen or under the stairs. There are also many other Feng Shui factors to consider but this is certainly an interesting area to explore if you wish to.

Summery of Crystal Grid Preparation:

1. Gather all your crystals and anything else you need together.

2. Cleanse the energy of the crystals and any other items to be used. Consecrate them if you wish and if you have not done so already.

3. Activate your crystals by programming them with your intention. Use either the Activation Wand, All-In-One or the Combination method.

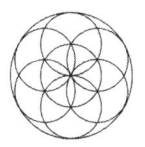

6

CRYSTAL GRID CARE & MAINTENANCE

Once you have a Crystal Grid set up and working, it will be broadcasting its energy 24/7 for you. Although you do not need to do anything more, there are some things you should do to make sure that your grid is working at its best.

Dusting Crystal Grids

If your Crystal Grid is left for at least a few weeks you will likely start to see dust building up around the crystals. When your crystals become dusty they are less effective. Dust is like stagnant energy, by cleaning your crystals and the surrounding surface you bring in fresh energy. Allowing your Crystal Grid to build up lots of dust around it could even stop it from working.

Cleaning a Crystal Grid can seem like a bit of work, but there is a way to do it that I find easier. First you need a dusting cloth. I recommend you use a lint free one. I find the best ones for cleaning crystals are the soft microfibre cloths that come with glasses, phones and computers. You can also use cloths that are designed for cleaning windows and glass. Just make sure they do not have any chemicals in them and are dry.

Here's a tip, there is a way to move the crystals without mixing up the stones. First move the crystals out of the way one by one but reproduce the same Crystal Grid design where you move them. This way it is easier to put them back where they were. You can also refer to this book as a guide. It is better if you can put the same crystal back into the same position it was in before. This is so that the energy pattern is the same as when you first made your grid.

When the crystals are out of the way you can now clean the surface and any templates the crystals were placed on. Then one by one, clean each crystal with the dry soft cloth. Do not use any cleaning products on crystals. Once free of dust you can place the crystals back where they were, on the now clean area.

Cleansing Crystal Grids

This is something you should consider if a Crystal Grid has been in place for over a month or so. The other reason you may want to energetically cleanse the crystals again is if you feel the Crystal Grid seems to have lost its effectiveness.

Crystals are very sensitive tools and while being placed in our Homes they will absorb energies that are not conductive to our original intention. When you cleanse the crystals that are part of an active Crystal Grid it does not remove the original program placed into them when it was activated. That is called Deactivation and we will get to how to do that later.

You do not need to move the crystals for this. There are ways to cleanse your Crystal Grid without touching the crystals directly. If you have your own preferred cleansing methods then please use those. It is much easier to use smudging, Palo Santo, Ting Shas or a Tibetan Singing Bowl as you do not need to move the crystals around. With incense methods you can waft the smoke around the area of the Crystal Grid with your hand or a feather. With Ting Shas or a Singing Bowl, simply hold them over the Crystal Grid and sound them as you would for cleansing crystals or a room. Another alternative is the following energy based technique, which uses Universal White Light but in a different way than before:

How To Cleanse Your Crystal Grid With Universal White Light

1. Place your hands palm down over the Crystal Grid. Get close but avoid touching the crystals if you can.

2. Close your eyes and visualise a beam of pure white light coming down from above, into your Crown Chakra (At the top of your head) down to the Heart Chakra (At the centre of your chest). Moving out along your arms and into your hands.

3. Visualise this white light shining down from the palms of your hands onto your Crystal Grid. See this Universal White Light in your mind's eye filling the crystals and surrounding them.

4. Focus on clearing the grid as you say out loud or in your head *"I cleanse, purify and rebalance this Crystal Grid of all negative, unbalanced or fear based energy, now"*

5. When you feel this has been done, open your eyes.

Copper Pyramids

I use Copper Pyramids to cleanse and rebalance my crystals all the time. Copper Pyramids focus energies but also purify and rebalance the energy of anything placed inside them. When crystals are combined with Copper something very magical seems to happen.

Copper Pyramids are not inexpensive devices but can be a way to save you having to worry about cleansing a Crystal Grid. Any Crystal Grid kept inside a Copper Pyramid will be cleansed and constantly protected from outside energies. You can make these pyramids yourself if you have the right tools or know someone who does welding. Ideally you will want to follow the dimensions of the Great Pyramid of Giza for maximum effect. The proportions of the Great Pyramid use very special angles, which relate to Sacred Geometry and the Earth.

You will need a Copper Pyramid that is big enough to place over the entire Crystal Grid. For a Copper Pyramid to work you will also need to align one of the four triangular sides with magnetic North. This charges the pyramid and connects it with the Earth's energy grid and magnetic field.

Deactivating a Crystal Grid

Once you are finished with a Crystal Grid, you will want to deactivate it and use the crystals for something else. It is vital that you cleanse and deprogram all the crystals. They will be holding your intentions, which could interfere with their use in the future. This could cause confused effects on other Crystal Grids you might use them in.

The crystals just keep doing their job until you tell them to stop. See it like a radio signal that just keeps broadcasting. When it is time and your crystals have finished their work, use the following method to deactivate the grid. It will cleanse and deprogram all the crystals and any other items used. This can of course be altered to use whichever cleansing method you prefer to use.

How To Deactivate a Crystal Grid

1. Start by removing all the crystals from their position within the Crystal Grid, along with any other items you used with it.

2. Hold all the crystals and items together in your hands if possible. If not you can work in batches. Close your eyes and take three deep breaths.

3. Now visualise a beam of pure white light coming down from above, into your Crown Chakra (At the top of your head) down to the Heart Chakra (At the centre of your chest). Moving out along your arms and into your hands.

4. See this Universal White Light in your mind's eye filling the crystals and items and surrounding them.

5. Focus on clearing everything as you say out loud or in your head *"I cleanse, purify and rebalance these crystals of all negative, unbalanced or fear based energies, now!"*

6. Then follow with *"I clear and remove all previous patterns and programs stored within this Crystal Grid, now!"*

7. When you feel this has been done, open your eyes.

Once this has been done your crystals and all other items are completely clear and deactivated. Everything is ready to be put away for now or used again for other Crystal Grids or whatever you want in the future.

7

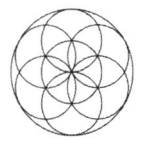

ENHANCING YOUR INTENTIONS

Now you know how to prepare, activate and maintain a Crystal Grid, there are a few things you may want to also do. Once your Crystal Grid is set up you might want to enhance its effects and bring the energy of your grid with you. These are just optional extra ways to help you get to your goals or support you on the journey.

The more you are focused on a goal or something you are trying to manifest, the more likely you are to see it happen. The Crystal Grid will be a reminder of your intention for the time being but it is not portable. Some people need reminders throughout the day. Some need to focus their mind daily to help them take the right actions and motivate themselves.

This chapter will look at ways to use crystals within your personal energy field or Aura. It will also look at other tools for your mind and spirit, which can help you towards your goals. Think about how the intention behind your Crystal Grid relates to these tools. How can you use one or more of these techniques in your daily life to keep you on the path to your desired outcome?

Pocket Crystals

Crystals are available in a variety of sizes and forms. Tumble Stones are one of the easiest and affordable ways to use the power of crystals in your daily life. You could also use small Crystal Points or Thumb Stones. Thumb Stones are small polished flat oval shaped stones with a carved recess to comfortably place your thumb in.

Look at the crystals that are included in your Crystal Grid. They all align with your intention and offer support for your journey. Clear Quartz is usually used for any intention because it is highly programmable. I include some of the key properties of the crystals for each grid to help you select a crystal. You may find you are naturally drawn to one of the crystals in the Crystal Grid already. Or you could use one of the substitute stones I suggest for the grid if you prefer.

Once you select a crystal, you will want to protect it by placing it in a small drawstring bag. Look for soft material, velvet or leather. Organza bags are the mesh material often used as gift bags when you purchase crystals online. These may look pretty but will not protect your crystal while you're carrying it about.

You can take this crystal with you by putting the bag in your pocket. Other ways are to place it inside your purse or wallet. Some women do not use the bag and place the Tumbled Stone inside the bottom of their bra. When carrying or wearing crystals regularly they will absorb all kinds of energies from you so will need clearing at least a few times a week to keep them working at their optimal level. This applies to all the other ways to use crystals in this chapter.

It can be helpful if the crystal you choose is also charged with your intention. Crystals will work for you without this but I find when you program a crystal you bring a laser like focus to it. The procedure is similar the one I have for activating your Crystal Grid. Here is a method for programming any crystal for your intention. This can also be used for the other options to enhance your Crystal Grids in this chapter.

Programming will imprint your energy and intention into the crystal. When you program a crystal you are communicating your clear intention so that it can help you. This does not limit the crystal in any way. You are not telling the crystal 'how' you want it to help you. Again you can come up with your own statement of intention or use the one that I suggest with the Crystal Grid you are working with.

How To Program a Crystal

1. Hold your cleansed crystal or crystals in your hands.

2. Sit for a few moments with your eyes closed. Get really clear about your intention.

3. Raise your crystal up in front of your Third Eye Chakra. Between and just above your eyes.

4. Focus on your desired result. Say to yourself or out loud a statement of your intention. You can use the one I have included with all Crystal Grids in this book or create your own: *"I program this crystal for..."* or *"I charge this Crystal to..."* or *"I ask this crystal to assist me with..."*

Crystal Bags & Pouches

Perhaps you wish to carry more than just one crystal? Maybe you want to have one each of the different crystals used in your Crystal Grid with you wherever you go? This can be done too.

As you will be keeping a group of crystals together it is best to use the polished Tumble Stones. These are less prone to chipping or damage. Decide on which stones you want to include in your crystal bag. Then select a soft and protective drawstring bag for them.

Cleanse and possibly program them for your intention. You can cleanse and program all the crystals you have chosen together at the same time. As with pocket crystals, you can take the bag with you anywhere. If you include a Clear Quartz crystal Tumble Stone, it will also enhance the energies of all the other stones. Some people like to include other symbolic items or herbs in these bags but it is not essential. This is sometimes called a Medicine Bag and can even be worn around the neck.

Quartz Crystal Points

As Clear Quartz Crystal Points are good to program and focus energies, they make good pocket crystals. You only need a small Crystal Point but avoid crystals that are too small, fragile or very narrow, as they are likely to break or damage. This will be a personal crystal that you will have with you all the time, so choose one that looks and feels right for you.

Cleanse and program the crystal for your needs and intention if you like. Place it in a small protective drawstring bag as with any pocket crystal. Some people prefer to only carry Tumble Stones, as they are more comfortable to put in their pocket. Another way you can use a Crystal Point is in the form of a pendant worn around the neck as a necklace.

Crystal Jewellery

Gemstone jewellery has been worn for its metaphysical power for thousands of years. You may already have something that you can wear which uses one of the crystals in your Crystal Grid. Many of the crystals featured in this book can be found as jewellery for men and women. Choose something you will wear daily, while your Crystal Grid is up and running. As before select stones from the crystals used in your Crystal Grid or the substitute stones.

You can wear crystal bracelets and necklaces very easily in your day to day life. Jewellery has symbolic meaning for many people. So if you do decide to get something new to work with your Crystal Grid, it will always remind you of your intention. Crystal jewellery does not need to be visible to work, you can discreetly wear a necklace.

Crystal Jewellery will also work like any personal crystal. It will allow you to access the energy of the crystal while you have it on your body and within your Aura. Just make sure you cleanse your jewellery and consider programming it for your specific intention.

Affirmations

Now we will look at other ways to work with and enhance your Crystal Grid's power. Affirmations are usually positive statements made out loud or in your head. These are similar to mantras as they are spoken multiple times. Either in set numbers like three or ten or over and over, countless times.

The idea is that affirmations help reprogram your mindset through the subconscious mind. Negative thinking and self talk does affect us. If you tell yourself you can't do something, over time you will start to believe it. You could see affirmations as counteracting this or reprogramming your mind. People also use affirmations to help manifest things through focused intent.

Although affirmations are not for everyone, many people use them successfully. You could create your own affirmations or find some online which are in alignment with the change you want to see in your life. Repeat these for a few minutes each morning and or before you go to bed. At the very least they will certainly keep you focused on your goal.

Visualisations

Visualisations are another well used meditation technique to bring about change and manifest different things. Like everything else in this book it will not do the work for you. Visualisation is a powerful way to focus the mind on the end result. It also builds up creative energy, which will help attract your desired outcome.

Some people find it hard to believe that our thoughts can really create our reality. This very book started out as a thought, an idea in my head. I wrote it down into words and then sketched a book cover idea in a note book. Here it is many months later in physical reality. Having a clear vision of what you want can only help you.

You may like to include a visualisation into your morning or bedtime routine. Focus on what it is you want to achieve with your Crystal Grid. Perhaps you can even sit near the Crystal Grid and meditate for a few minutes each day on your intention. Try to see and feel what it would be like to have the desired result now. If you can bring in emotion of how good it will feel, this will super charge your visualisations even more. You can also combine this with affirmations. The words may also help stop your mind from wandering. If it does, just bring it back to your original intention.

Vision Boards

Vision boards are a collection of images and words related to your goals and aspirations. You can search for images online or use catalogues and magazines. You want images that represent your desired outcome. There are also lots of inspiring quotes and affirmations, which can be included in your vision board.

Once you find the images you want, print them out if needed and pin or stick them, collage style to a piece of card or a cork pin board. This can be added to or changed over time. Although vision boards are usually a collection of many goals you can make smaller and more focused ones.

Ideally you want this visual representation to be hung up somewhere you will see it every day. The vision board helps you stay motivated and focused on your goal. Look at it whenever you need to remind yourself of what you want to manifest. It can also give you ideas for visualisations or be used as a focal point in your meditations.

Deprogramming Crystals

Before we move on, I want to show you something many books do not mention. If you have programmed a crystal or some crystal jewellery, you can also deprogram it at any time. Once you have finished working with your stone, you can clear it of any programs or intentions it carries by following the steps below.

This process is similar to deactivating a Crystal Grid. It is certainly something you will want to do after your Crystal Grid has completed its job and all the crystals have been put away. Gather any programmed crystals or jewellery that you carried or wore together and cleanse them first.

How To Deprogram a Crystal

1. Hold your cleansed crystal, crystals or jewellery in your hands.

2. Raise this up in front of your Third Eye Chakra. Between and just above your eyes.

3. Say to yourself or out loud: *"I cancel, clear and delete this crystal of all previous programs or intentions, now!"*

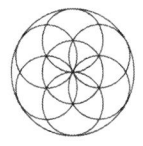

8

SIMPLE CRYSTAL GRIDS

Now that you know why Crystal Grids work and how to set them up, I want to show you a really simple and easy grid. This super simple Crystal Grid can be customised and used for any purpose. The geometric pattern it uses is the Flower of Life, which you may remember from the Sacred Geometry Reference Guide earlier.

The Flower of Life is found all around the world, painted onto walls and etched into stone. The symbol is said to contain all other shapes and forms of Sacred Geometry. Many believe it represents the whole Universe.

The Flower of Life has become one of the most used designs for Crystal Grids today. It is a universal symbol and serves as a multi purpose grid layout. It brings in cosmic energies and assists in manifesting anything.

The other benefit of the following Crystal Grid is that it can be easily formed with just a few crystals. Each of these Crystal Grids uses six Clear Quartz Crystal Points and one Central Stone. The Central Stone could be a Standing Crystal Point or other recommended Central Stone form. You could also use a medium or large sized Tumble Stone. I have also included some options for alternative crystals for the Central Stone to give you more choice.

You can use these Crystal Grids when you are in a hurry. It may take time to find all the crystals needed for the more complex Crystal Grids in the next chapter of this book. One of these grids could be set up in the meantime. Once you have printed off the Flower of Life template from the link below and have six Quartz Crystal Points, you only need to find one other crystal.

These Crystal Grids are quick, easy to make and effective. They may not be as powerful as the more advanced Crystal Grids, only because they do not use as many different types of crystal. More crystals bring more types of energy in to help, which also has a more synergistic effect. Try these grids and see what you think, you may find they work just as well for you. They are ideal for when something comes up and you need to set up a Crystal Grid straight away. To see some finished photo examples of the Crystal Grids from this book, please visit the Resources page of my website and look under the Crystal Grids section.

The '**Crystal Grid Template A**' is used for all of these simple grids and can be found in the printable Crystal Grid Template file below. Print this on some good quality card if you want the template to last a long time. If you do not have access to a printer, the Flower of Life is probably the most easy to find and useful of Crystal Grid Templates to invest in.

Please do not share this link with anyone. If for any reason the link is not working, please wait a few hours and try again later. If it is still not working please contact me through my website, email or on social media.

www.ethanlazzerini.com/grid-templates

SIMPLE ABUNDANCE CRYSTAL GRID

This is a simple Crystal Grid for creating abundance, prosperity and wealth. You can use it to help create a better financial flow in your life. It may lead you towards ways of increasing or creating a more steady income. Write an affirmation of your intention on a small piece of paper. Fold this and place it under the Central Stone.

Tip: You could also use an image to illustrate the type of abundance you want to manifest. Place this with the note under the Central Stone.

Crystals Used:

1 Large or Medium Citrine
6 Clear Quartz Crystal Points

Regular Crystal Grid Template: A

Sacred Geometry Meaning:

The Flower of Life supports all purposes and connects with the Universe. It is a tool for manifesting.

(1) Central Stone: Citrine

In position 1 place a large or medium sized Citrine crystal in the centre of the grid. Citrine attracts abundance and helps create a successful mindset. This crystal can be substituted with Yellow Jade, Green Jade, Green Aventurine or Pyrite.

(2) Support Stones: Clear Quartz

In position 2 arrange the six Clear Quartz Crystal Points, pointing outwards. The Clear Quartz crystals will focus, direct and amplify the energies and intention of the grid.

Intention Statement:

"*I program this Crystal Grid to attract abundance and prosperity into my life*".

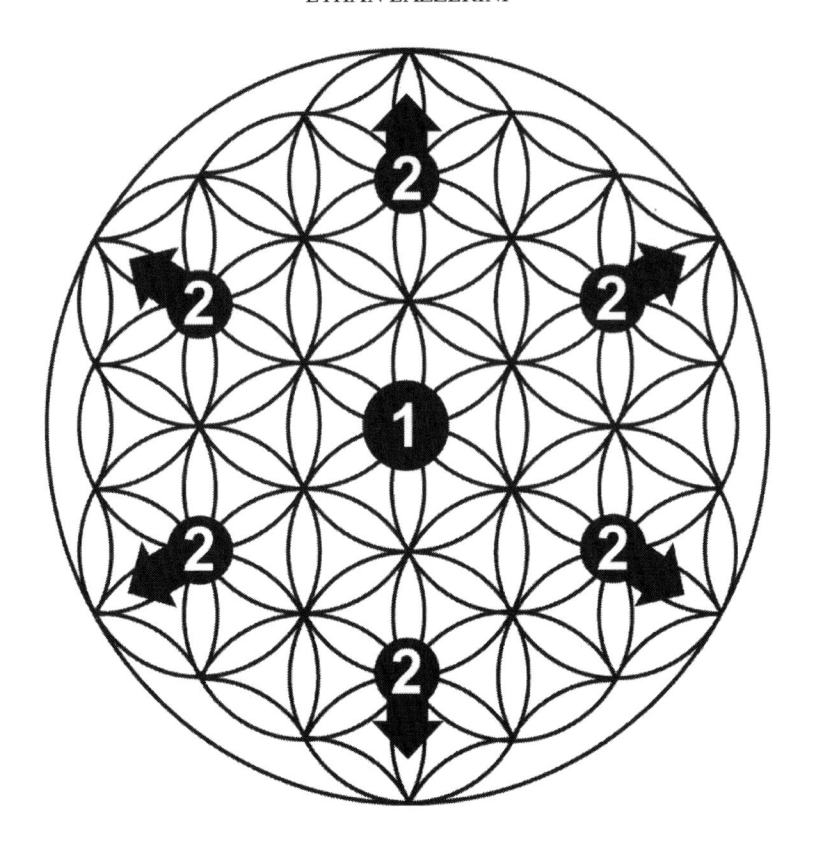

SIMPLE HEALING CRYSTAL GRID

This is a simple Crystal Grid to bring better health, wellness and support the healing process. You can use this grid on yourself or for someone else requesting the healing, anywhere in the world. Write an affirmation of your intention, including the name of the person needing healing on a small piece of paper. Fold this and place it under the Central Stone.

Tip: You could also place a photo of the person in good health with the note under the Central Stone.

Crystals Used:

1 Large or Medium Amazonite
6 Clear Quartz Crystal Points

Regular Crystal Grid Template: A

Sacred Geometry Meaning:

The Flower of Life supports all purposes and connects with the Universe.

(1) Central Stone: Amazonite

In position 1 place a large or medium sized Amazonite crystal in the centre of the grid. Amazonite brings healing energy and balances your Aura. This crystal can be substituted with Bloodstone, Chevron Amethyst (also known as Banded Amethyst or Dream Amethyst), Goldstone (also known as Gold Stone) or Faden Quartz.

(2) Support Stones: Clear Quartz

In position 2 arrange the six Clear Quartz Crystal Points, pointing outwards. The Clear Quartz crystals will focus, direct and amplify the energies and intention of the grid.

Intention Statement:

"I program this Crystal Grid to restore health and bring healing to .... if it be for their highest and greatest good".

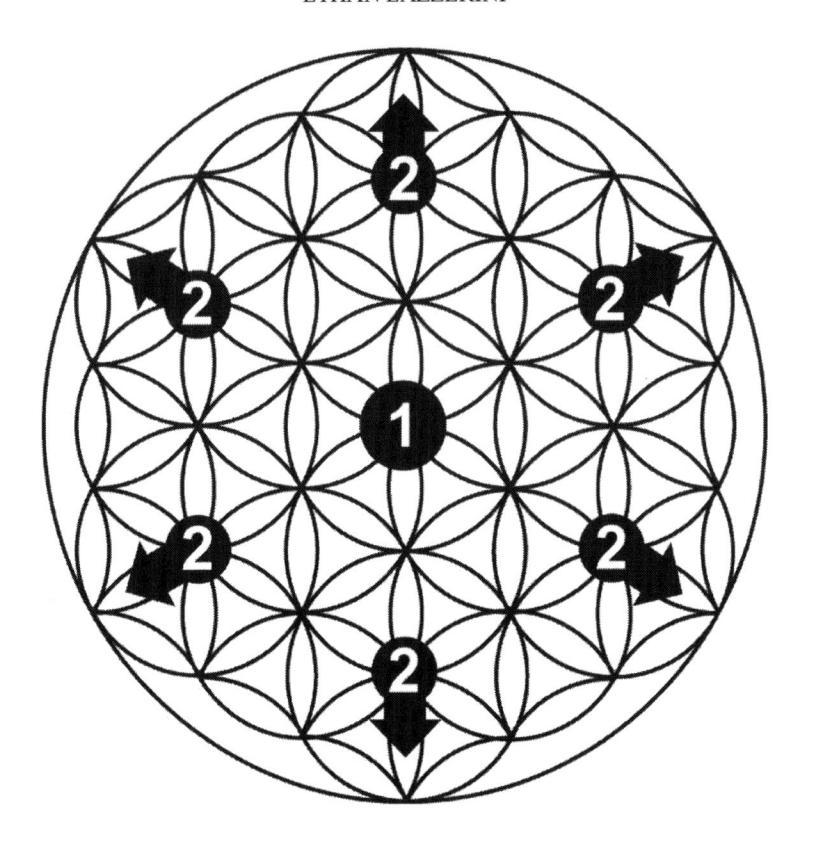

SIMPLE PROTECTION CRYSTAL GRID

This is a quick and simple Crystal Grid for general psychic protection. Use it to protect yourself, a family member or someone who has asked for your help. Write an affirmation of your intention, including the name or names of those needing protection on a small piece of paper. Fold this and place it under the Central Stone.

Tip: If this grid has been made for someone else you could also use a photo of them. Place this with the note under the Central Stone.

Crystals Used:

1 Large or Medium Hematite
6 Clear Quartz Crystal Points

Regular Crystal Grid Template: A

Sacred Geometry Meaning:

The Flower of Life supports all purposes and connects with the Universe.

(1) Central Stone: Hematite

In position 1 place a large or medium sized Hematite in the centre of the grid. Hematite shields from and neutralises harmful energy, it also strengthens the Aura. This crystal can be substituted with Black Tourmaline or Black Obsidian.

(2) Support Stones: Clear Quartz

In position 2 arrange the six Clear Quartz Crystal Points, pointing outwards. The Clear Quartz crystals will focus, direct and amplify the energies and intention of the grid.

Intention Statement:

"*I program this Crystal Grid to protect .... from all forms of harm*".

SIMPLE RELATIONSHIPS CRYSTAL GRID

This is a simple Crystal Grid for enhancing loving relationships or creating better family harmony. You can use it to help calm and resolve relationship issues. This grid can also balance a relationship, heal rifts and bring forgiveness to hurt feelings. Write an affirmation of your intention on a small piece of paper. Fold this and place it under the Central Stone.

Tip: You could also use a photo of you and your partner or a happy family photo. Place this with the note under the Central Stone.

Crystals Used:

1 Large or Medium Rose Quartz
6 Clear Quartz Crystal Points

Regular Crystal Grid Template: A

Sacred Geometry Meaning:

The Flower of Life supports all purposes and connects with the Universe.

(1) Central Stone: Rose Quartz

In position 1 place a large or medium sized Rose Quartz crystal in the centre of the grid. Rose Quartz brings a calming, loving and compassionate energy. This crystal can be substituted with Rhodonite, Pink Opal or Mangano Calcite.

(2) Support Stones: Clear Quartz

In position 2 arrange the six Clear Quartz Crystal Points, pointing outwards. The Clear Quartz crystals will focus, direct and amplify the energies and intention of the grid.

Intention Statement:

"*I program this Crystal Grid for loving relationships and harmony with .... if that be for the highest and greatest good of all*".

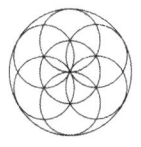

9

MORE ADVANCED CRYSTAL GRIDS

These Crystal Grids are more complex and generally will use more different types of crystals. Their design will draw on more geometric shapes. You will need to look for Central Stones that are larger in size or have more mass to give the grid more power. These Crystal Grids seem to have more energy and a higher impact on situations.

Your Central Stone should be in one of the powerful forms listed earlier in Chapter 4. As with the Simple Crystal Grids I have also included substitute crystals if needed. These will have a slightly different energy but are still in alignment with the core intention of the Crystal Grid. You can use any of these instead.

All the Crystal Grid Templates used here can be found in the free printable Crystal Grids Templates file at the link below:

www.ethanlazzerini.com/grid-templates

ABUNDANCE & PROSPERITY CRYSTAL GRID

This regular Crystal Grid can be used to help bring more abundance and increased prosperity into your life. Use this grid to support healthy finances and to balance or increase your income flow. A good one for supporting career or business success. Write an affirmation of your intention on a small piece of paper. Fold this and place it under the Central Stone.

Tip: You could also place a Lucky Chinese Coin on top of the folded note to attract wealth and prosperity. These are antique or replica coins with a square hole through the middle. Make sure the side with the four characters is facing up.

Crystals Used:

1 Large Citrine
3 Yellow Jade Tumble Stones
3 Pyrite Tumble Stones
8 Clear Quartz Crystal Points

Regular Crystal Grid Template: B

Sacred Geometry Meaning:

The Octagram taps into abundance, prosperity and supports growth. The Flower of Life helps with manifesting.

(1) Central Stone: Citrine

In position 1 place a large Citrine crystal. Citrine attracts wealth and prosperity. This crystal can be substituted with Tiger's Eye.

(2) Inner Support Stones: Yellow Jade

In position 2 place the three Yellow Jade Tumble Stones. Yellow Jade is a good stone for abundance. These crystals can be substituted with Green Jade, Green Aventurine or Moss Agate.

(3) Inner Support Stones: Pyrite

In position 3 place the three Pyrite Tumble Stones. Pyrite is used for attracting prosperity. These crystals can be substituted with Lodestone or Tiger's Eye, if not already used.

(4) Outer Support Stones: Clear Quartz

In position 4 arrange the eight Clear Quartz Crystal Points, pointing outwards. The Clear Quartz crystals will focus, direct and amplify the energies and intention of the grid.

Intention Statement:

"I program this Crystal Grid to attract increased abundance and prosperity into my life".

ALL PURPOSE CRYSTAL GRID

This all Quartz regular Crystal Grid can be used for almost any purpose you can think of. A good all-rounder. The crystals and the arrangement will support any specific intention or goal not listed in this book. This is a good one to experiment with and begin creating your own more personalised grids. Write an affirmation of your intention on a small piece of paper. Fold this and place it under the Central Stone.

Tip: You could also include a photo of a person or map under the Central Stone if needed. Or use an image to represent your desired outcome.

Crystals Used:

1 Large Clear Quartz Crystal
12 Clear Quartz Crystal Points

Regular Crystal Grid Template: A

Sacred Geometry Meaning:

The Flower of Life supports all purposes and connects with the Universe. It also helps with manifesting things.

(1) Central Stone: Clear Quartz

In position 1 place a large Clear Quartz crystal. All the Clear Quartz crystals used in this grid will focus, direct and amplify the energies and intention of the grid.

(2) Inner Support Stones: Clear Quartz

In position 2 arrange six Clear Quartz Crystal Points, pointing outwards.

(3) Outer Support Stones: Clear Quartz

In position 3 arrange six Clear Quartz Crystal Points, pointing outwards.

Intention Statement:

"*I program this Crystal Grid to .... if that be for the highest and greatest good of all*".

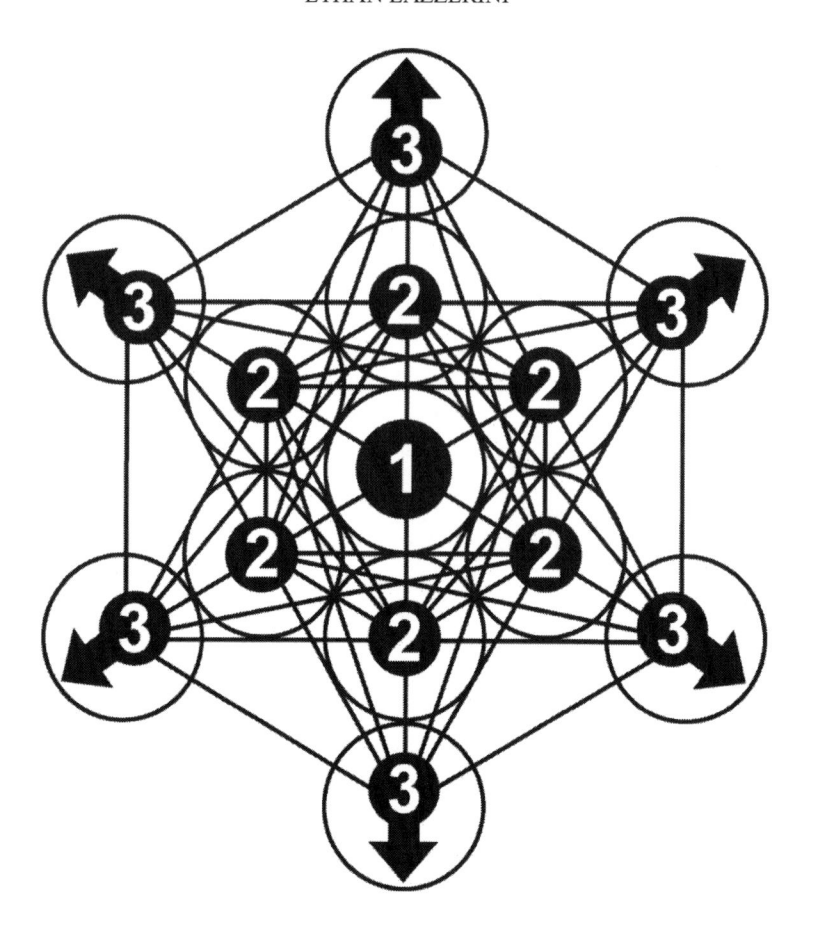

ANGELIC CONNECTION CRYSTAL GRID

This regular Crystal Grid can be used for connecting and working more closely with your Angels. The grid assists in communication with the Angelic Realm, Guardian Angels and the Archangels. It acts as an anchor point for angelic energy. Write an affirmation of your intention on a small piece of paper. Fold this and place it under the Central Stone.

Tip: You could use a carved Quartz crystal in the shape of an Angel or pair of wings as your Central Stone for this one.

Crystals Used:

1 Large Angel Aura Crystal
6 Celestite Tumble Stones
6 Danburite Crystals

Regular Crystal Grid Template: C

Sacred Geometry Meaning:

Metatron's Cube is used for connection with the Angelic Realms, protection and accessing spiritual wisdom.

(1) Central Stone: Angel Aura

In position 1 place a large Angel Aura crystal (also known as Opal Aura). This high vibration Platinum enhanced crystal connects you with your Angels. This crystal can be substituted with an Angel Phantom Quartz crystal (also known as Amphibole Quartz). Or use a Clear Quartz Crystal.

(2) Inner Support Stones: Celestite

In position 2 place six Celestite Tumble Stones. Celestite (also known as Celestine) connects with the Angelic Realms. These crystals can be substituted with Angelite.

(3) Outer Support Stones: Danburite

In position 3 arrange six Danburite Tumble Stones or Danburite Crystal Points, pointing outwards. Danburite anchors powerful angelic energy and light. These crystals can be substituted with Clear Quartz Crystal Points.

Intention Statement:

"I program this Crystal Grid to bring support, messages and guidance from the Angels".

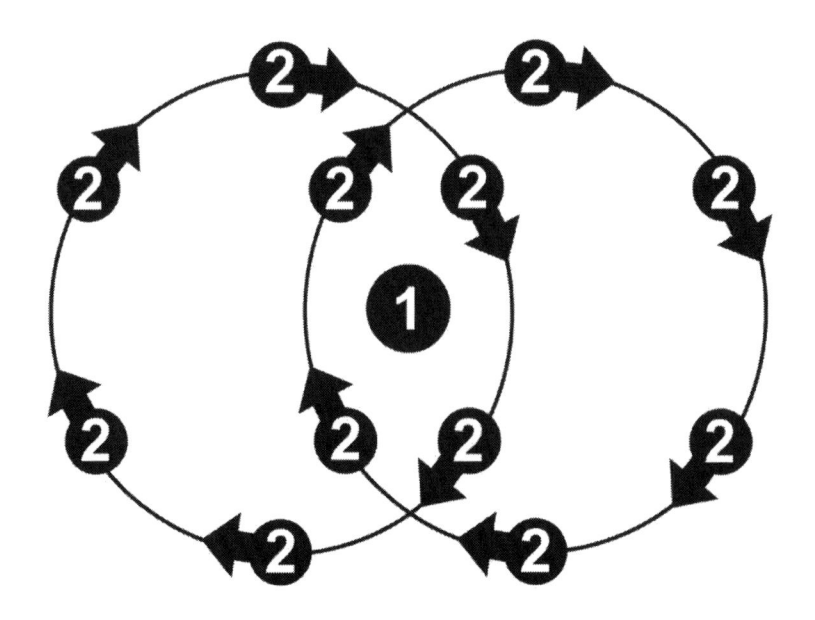

ATTRACT A LOVING PARTNER CRYSTAL GRID

This regular Crystal Grid can be used to help attract a loving romantic partner into your life. It can assist you in finding someone who is also seeking a committed relationship. It is not advisable to use anyone's name in the intention statement to respect others free will. Write an affirmation of your intention on a small piece of paper. Fold this and place it under the Central Stone.

Tip: You could use a heart shaped Rose Quartz crystal as the Central Stone for this one.

Crystals Used:

1 Large Rose Quartz Crystal
12 Clear Quartz Crystal Points

Regular Crystal Grid Template: D

Sacred Geometry Meaning:

The two Circles represent union and commitment. The Vesica Piscis opens the door to new experiences and opportunities.

(1) Central Stone: Rose Quartz

In position 1 place a large Rose Quartz crystal. Rose Quartz opens the Heart Chakra and helps attract loving relationships. This crystal can be substituted with Mangano Calcite, Rhodonite or a Rose Aura Crystal.

(2) Support Stones: Clear Quartz

In position 2 arrange the twelve Clear Quartz Crystal Points. Six Crystal Points per circle, pointing clockwise. The Clear Quartz Crystals will focus, direct and amplify the energies and intention of the grid.

Intention Statement:

"*I program this Crystal Grid to attract a loving, committed partner into my life. If that be for my highest and greatest good and the highest and greatest good of all*".

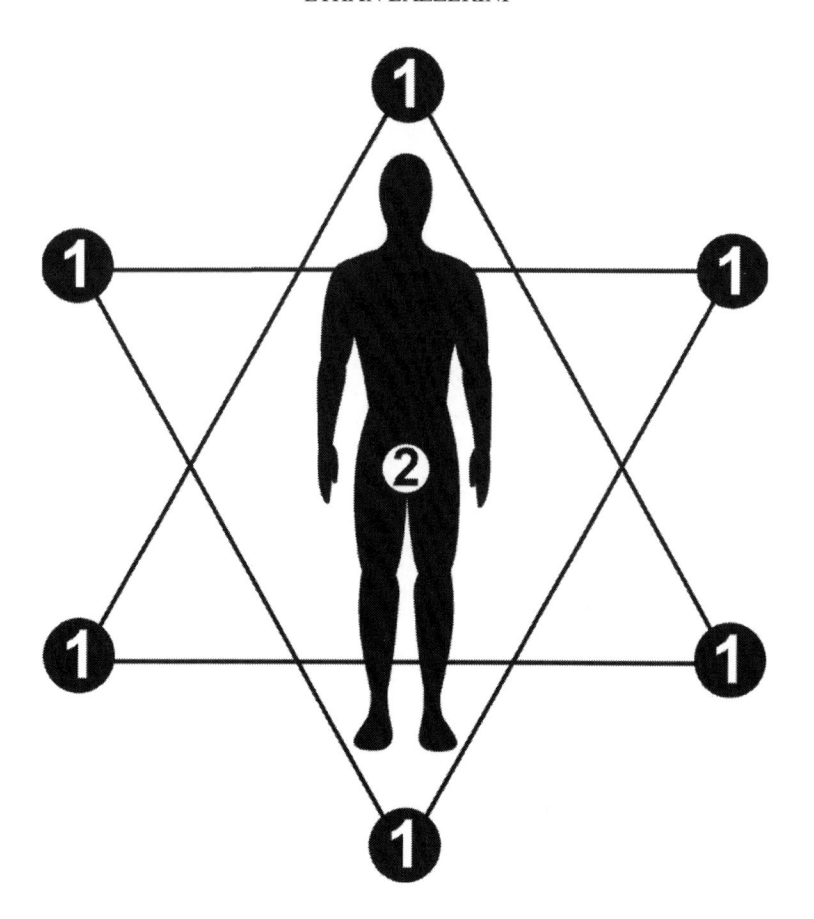

AURA BALANCING CRYSTAL GRID

This Body Crystal Grid layout is used to balance the energy and layers of the Aura. The Root Chakra crystal will help anchor the Aura. When your Aura is too large, you can take on everyone else's energy and emotions. When it is too close to the body, you may feel invisible to others or opportunities will pass you by. Use the All-In-One method of activation.

Tip: Use different coloured Fluorite crystals. Or crystals with a mixture of at least two colours. Multicoloured Fluorite is also known as Rainbow Fluorite.

Crystals Used:

6 Fluorite Tumble Stones or Octahedron Crystals
1 Hematite Tumble Stone

Body Crystal Grid

Sacred Geometry Meaning:

The Star of David brings balance and harmony.

(1) Support Stones: Fluorite

In position 1 arrange the six Fluorite Tumble Stones or natural Fluorite Octahedron Crystals. Fluorite balances all the layers of the Aura. This crystal can be substituted with Ametrine or Amazonite.

(2) Chakra Crystal: Hematite

Lay down within the grid. In position 2 place the Hematite Tumble Stone on your Root Chakra. This is at the base of the spine. You can place it on the body or under you. Hematite grounds the Aura and strengthens it. This crystal can be substituted with Red Jasper or Smoky Quartz.

Close your eyes and take some deep breaths. Lay here for about 10 to 15 minutes. Take your time before getting up again.

Intention Statement:

"I program this Crystal Grid to balance my energy and all layers of my Aura".

AURA CLEARING CRYSTAL GRID

This Body Crystal Grid layout is used to cleanse the Aura of negative or harmful energies. It will draw out any energies that do not belong to you or serve your highest good. Use this Crystal Grid whenever you feel weighed down after a stressful or bad day. It will detoxify, cleanse and refresh your energy field. Use the All-In-One method of activation.

Tip: Doing this one sitting down will save a lot of space. Just make sure your whole body is within the six crystals.

Crystals Used:

6 Black Tourmaline Crystal Points

Body Crystal Grid

Sacred Geometry Meaning:

The Star of David brings balance and protection.

(1) Support Stones: Black Tourmaline

In position 1 arrange six Black Tourmaline Crystal Points or Black Tourmaline Double Terminated Crystals, pointing outwards. Black Tourmaline absorbs and neutralises negative energies. These crystals can be substituted with Tourmalinated Quartz, natural or polished Selenite Wands, Citrine or Smoky Quartz Crystal Points. Make sure they are pointing outwards.

Sit cross legged or in a lotus position within the centre of the six crystals. Close your eyes and take some deep breaths. Sit here for about 10 to 15 minutes. Take your time before getting up again.

Intention Statement:

"*I program this Crystal Grid to cleanse my Aura of all negative, harmful or unbalanced energies or any energies within or around my Aura that do not serve my highest and greatest good*".

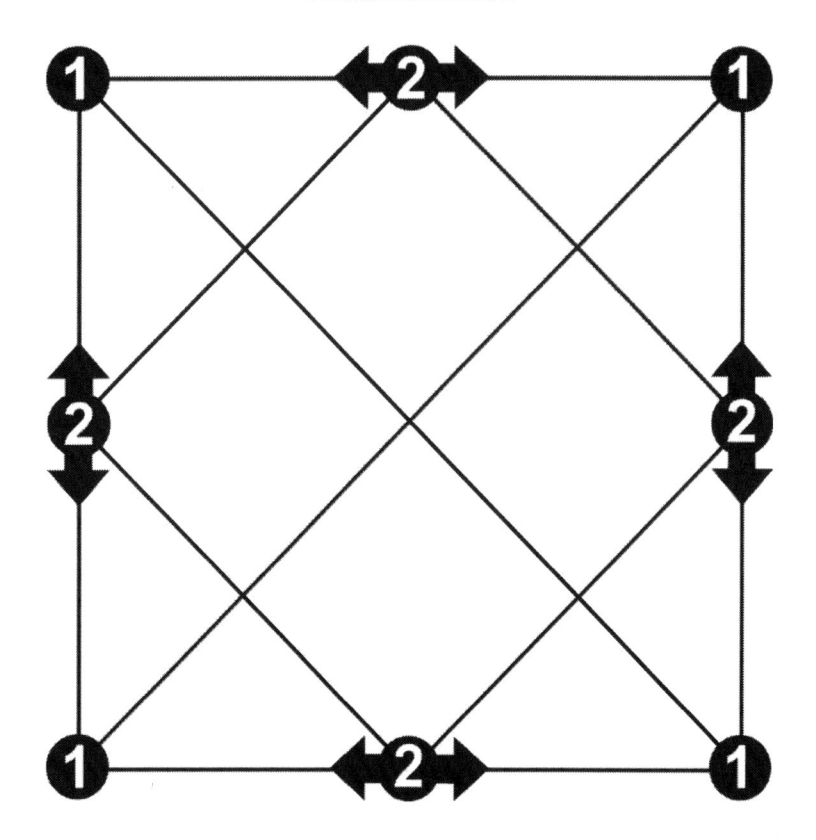

CLEANSE HOME CRYSTAL GRID

This Location Crystal Grid can be used to cleanse the energy of your Home or just one room. The crystals used in this grid work to help keep your space clear of negative, harmful or out of balance energies. It is good to use if the atmosphere feels heavy, if there has been a lot of illness or a run of bad luck. It also helps reduce any negative energies building up in the future by trapping and absorbing them. If gridding the entire Home, the ground floor is best for grid placement. Use the All-In-One method of activation.

Tip: You may still want to cleanse your Home every two or three months to help keep the crystals working at their best.

Crystals Used:

4 Large Black Tourmaline Crystal Points or Tumble Stones
4 Natural or Polished Selenite Wands

Location Crystal Grid

Sacred Geometry Meaning:

The Cross protects against negative energies. The Square and Diamond offer environmental support from all directions.

(1) Support Stones: Black Tourmaline

In position 1 place four Black Tourmaline crystals at the four corners of your Home or room. If using any type of Crystal Points, have them pointing outwards to form the cross. Black Tourmaline grounds, absorbs and neautralises negative energies. These stones can be substituted with Tourmalinated Quartz, Smoky Quartz Crystals or Snowflake Obsidian.

(2) Support Stones: Selenite

In position 2 place the four natural or polished Selenite Wands. These should lay flush against the walls. These crystals will also absorb and purify negative or harmful energies. These crystals may be substituted with Clear Quartz Crystal Points or Double Terminated Clear Quartz Crystals.

Intention Statement:

"I program this Crystal Grid to continuously cleanse, purify and rebalance the energy of my ....".

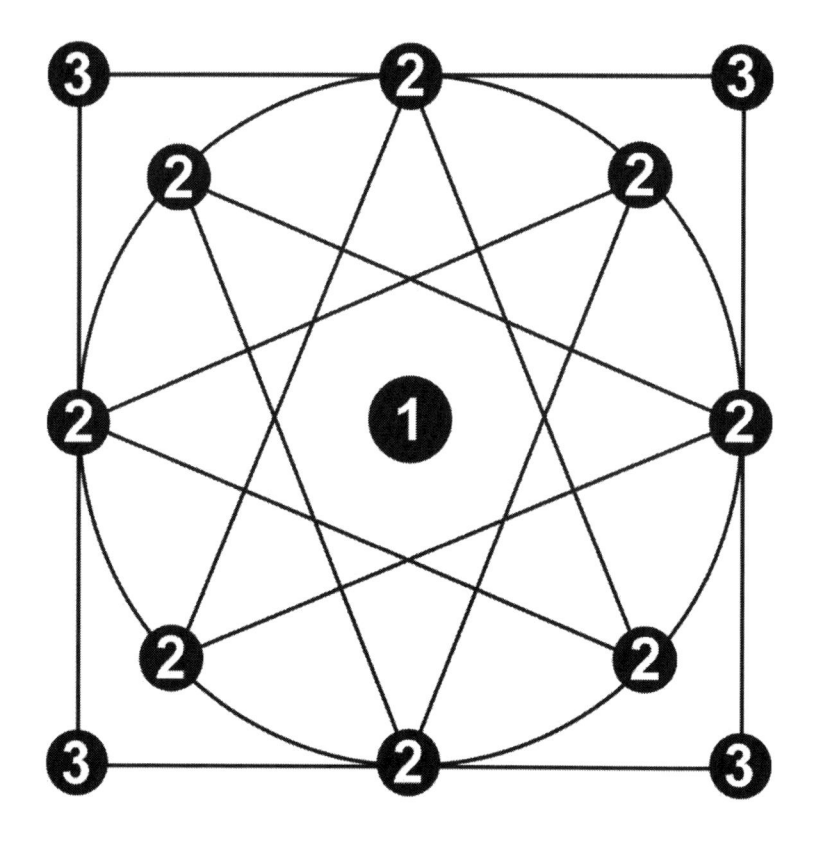

CONFIDENCE & COURAGE CRYSTAL GRID

This Regular Crystal Grid can be used to help you build your self confidence and give you more courage. Use this grid if you feel you are blocked by your fears or lack self belief in your abilities or self worth. Always follow through with action steps to develop your self confidence. Write an affirmation of your intention on a small piece of paper. Fold this and place it under the Central Stone.

Tip: You could also benefit from wearing Tiger's Eye in the form of a bracelet, pendant or carry a Tumble Stone in your pocket with you every day.

Crystals Used:

1 Large Tiger's Eye
8 Bronzite Tumble Stones
4 Carnelian Tumble Stones

Regular Crystal Grid Template: E

Sacred Geometry Meaning:

The Square brings inner strength. The Circle offers protection. The Octagram supports personal growth and builds determination.

(1) Central Stone: Tiger's Eye

In position 1 place a large Tiger's Eye crystal. Tiger's Eye is a confidence booster. This crystal can be substituted with a Citrine or a Clear Quartz Crystal.

(2) Inner Support Stones: Bronzite

In position 2 arrange the eight Bronzite Tumble Stones. Bronzite builds confidence and determination. These crystals can be substituted with Mahogany Obsidian Tumble Stones or Arrowheads, pointing outwards.

(3) Outer Support Stones: Carnelian

In position 3 arrange the four Carnelian Tumble Stones, the more red the better. Carnelian and especially Red Carnelian (also known as Blood of Isis) helps empower you. These crystals can be substituted with Sunstone or Hematite.

Intention Statement:

"I program this Crystal Grid to help me build self confidence and increase my courage".

EARTH HEALING CRYSTAL GRID

This Regular Crystal Grid can be used to bring healing to the Planet or any location around the world. These crystals bring in streams of healing light, compassion and cleansing energy. Use to bring spiritual support to areas of conflict or natural disasters. Write an affirmation of your intention on a small piece of paper. Fold this and place it under the Central Stone. You can also use a map of the location or a photo of Planet Earth, respectively.

Tip: You could use a Crystal Sphere or Crystal Heart for the Central Stone in this grid. Use a Crystal Merkaba for raising the vibration of the planet or an area.

Crystals Used:

1 Large Amazonite
6 Rose Quartz Tumble Stones
9 Amethyst Tumble Stones or Crystal Points

Regular Crystal Grid Template: F

Sacred Geometry Meaning:

The Flower of Life brings balance and harmony. The Enneagram supports peace, unity and compassion.

(1) Central Stone: Amazonite

In position 1 place a large Amazonite crystal. Amazonite brings healing and balances energies. This crystal can be substituted with Green Fluorite or Clear Quartz.

(2) Inner Support Stones: Rose Quartz

In position 2 arrange the six Rose Quartz Tumble Stones. Rose Quartz brings healing and compassion. These crystals can be substituted with Pink Opal, Rhodonite or Amazonite, if not already used in the centre.

(3) Outer Support Stones: Amethyst

In position 3 arrange the nine Amethyst Tumble Stones. Or if using Amethyst Crystal Points, have them pointing outwards. Amethyst transmutes negative energy and anchors spiritual energy. These crystals can be substituted with Selenite, Lapis Lazuli or Clear Quartz.

Intention Statement:

"*I program this Crystal Grid to bring healing, love and peace to .... if that be for the highest and greatest good of all*".

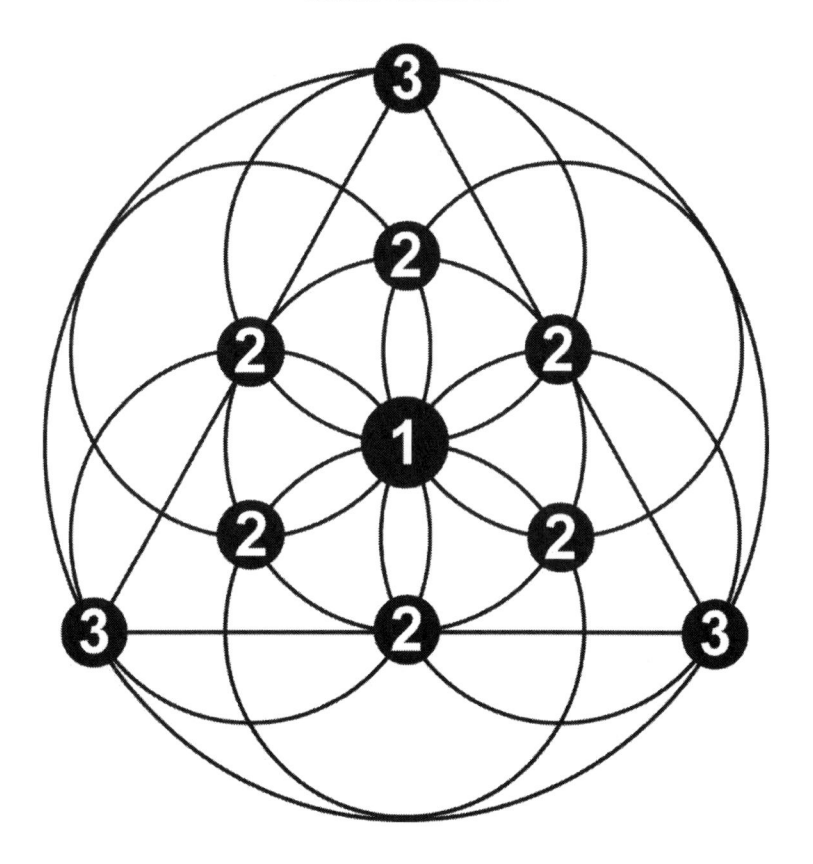

FAITH & HOPE CRYSTAL GRID

This Regular Crystal Grid will help increase your faith and bring hope. Use it when you feel like giving up on something or when you lack faith that a situation will ever improve. This Crystal Grid will help chase away feelings of doubt and fear and instill trust that things will work out for the best. Write an affirmation of your intention on a small piece of paper. Fold this and place it under the Central Stone.

Tip: You could use a Crystal Pyramid for the Central Stone to help increase divine connection and to raise your vibration.

Crystals Used:

1 Large Angel Aura
6 Tiger's Eye Tumble Stones
3 Turquoise Tumble Stones

Regular Crystal Grid Template: G

Sacred Geometry Meaning:

The Seed of Life supports growth and new beginnings. The Triangle increases divine connection and raises energy.

(1) Central Stone: Angel Aura

In position 1 place a large Angel Aura crystal (also known as Opal Aura). Angel Aura increases Faith and optimism. This crystal can be substituted with Clear Quartz.

(2) Inner Support Stones: Tiger's Eye

In position 2 arrange the six Tiger's Eye Tumble Stones. Tiger's Eye encourages positive thinking and faith. These crystals can be substituted with Sunstone or Goldstone (also known as Gold Stone).

(3) Outer Support Stones: Turquoise

In position 3 arrange the three Turquoise Tumble Stones. Turquoise brings faith and absorbs worries. These crystals can be substituted with Smoky Quartz or Healer's Gold (also known as Apache Gold). If using Crystal Points, have them point outwards.

Intention Statement:

"I program this Crystal Grid to strengthen my faith and bring me hope".

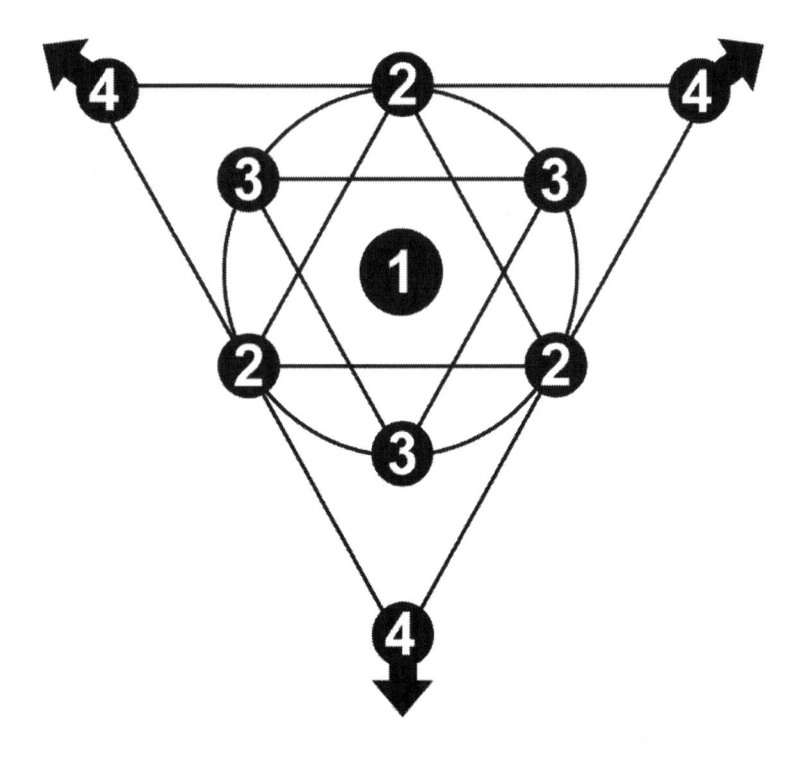

HEALING CRYSTAL GRID

This Regular Crystal Grid can be used to send healing energy to someone. The healing triangle will bring in multiple rays of healing light to those in need. It can be used on yourself or anyone that requests healing over a period of time. Use it when you are ill or after an operation to support the healing process. Write an affirmation of your intention on a small piece of paper. Fold this and place it under the Central Stone.

Tip: You could also use a photo of yourself or the person needing healing in good health. Place this with the note under the Central Stone.

Crystals Used:

1 Large Amazonite
3 Bloodstone Tumble Stones
3 Lapis Lazuli Tumble Stones
3 Clear Quartz Crystal Points

Regular Crystal Grid Template: H

Sacred Geometry Meaning:

The Triangle and Star of David balance energy and anchor divine light. The Circle supports renewal and gives protection.

(1) Central Stone: Amazonite

In position 1 place a large Amazonite crystal. Amazonite brings healing and balances energies. This crystal can be substituted with Rose Quartz or Clear Quartz.

(2) Inner Support Stones: Bloodstone

In position 2 arrange the three Bloodstone Tumble Stones. Bloodstone supports physical healing. These crystals can be substituted with Hematite, Magnetic Hematite or Goldstone (also known as Gold Stone).

(3) Inner Support Stones: Lapis Lazuli

In position 3 arrange the three Lapis Lazuli Tumble Stones. Lapis Lazuli brings spiritual healing and protection. These crystals can be substituted with Amethyst or Chevron Amethyst (also known as Banded Amethyst or Dream Amethyst).

(4) Outer Support Stones: Clear Quartz

In position 4 arrange the three Clear Quartz Crystal Points, pointing outwards. Clear Quartz draws off negative energy.

Intention Statement:

"I program this Crystal Grid to bring health & healing to .... if that be for the highest and greatest good".

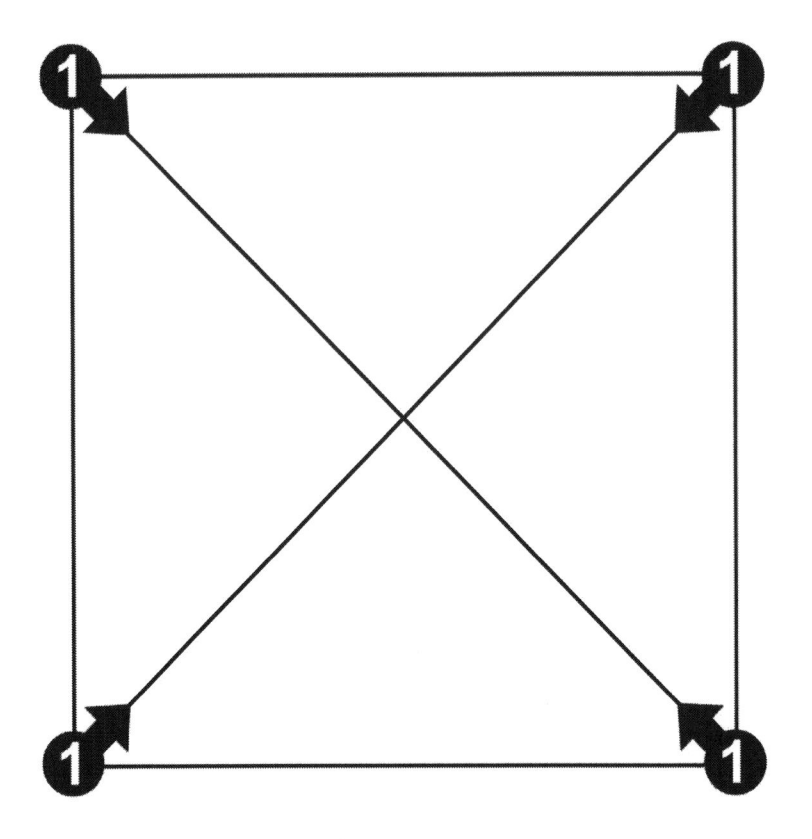

HOME BLESSING CRYSTAL GRID

This Location Crystal Grid can be used to bless your Home or just one room. The grid brings in positive high vibration spiritual energies to the location and those that live there. Blessing your Home keeps away negative or unwanted energies and welcomes new opportunities to enter. You can bless your Home when you move into a new place or at any time you wish. If gridding the entire Home, the ground floor is best for grid placement. The crystals can be removed after a week or left in place. Use the All-In-One method of activation.

Tip: For best effect you should cleanse the space first before placing the crystals. Burn Sage, Palo Santo or Sandalwood.

Crystals Used:

4 Large Citrine Crystal Points

Location Crystal Grid

Sacred Geometry Meaning:

The Square offers support from all directions. The Cross anchors spiritual energies into the Physical World.

(1) Support Stones: Citrine

In position 1 place four large Citrine Crystal Points in the four corners of your Home or room. Have them pointing inwards to form the cross. You could also use upright Standing Crystal Points instead. Citrine brings positive energies and abundance.

These crystals can be substituted with golden Rutilated Quartz (also known as Angel Hair Quartz), Sunstone, Ammolite (Iridescent Ammonite) or Clear Quartz Crystal Points.

Intention Statement:

"I program this Crystal Grid to bring an abundance of blessings and high vibration positive energy into my ....".

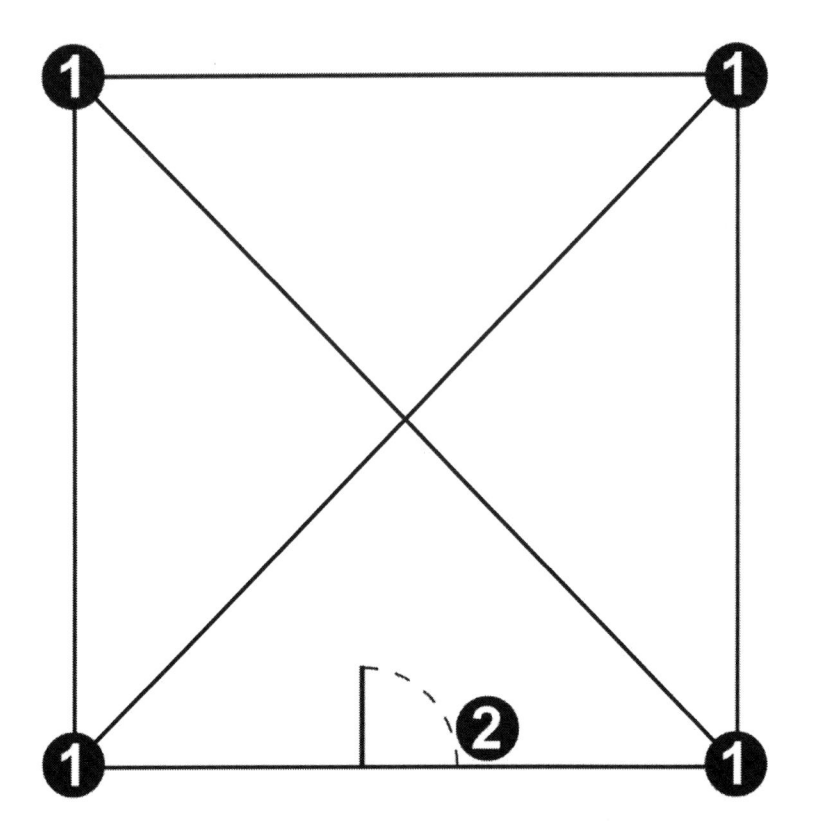

HOME PROTECTION CRYSTAL GRID

This Location Crystal Grid can be used to protect your Home or just one room. The crystals act like sentinels that protect the energy of your space. They ward off negative energy from entering and surround the location with a wall of powerful protection. You can leave it up or use it when you feel that you need extra protection. For gridding the entire Home, the ground floor is best for grid placement. Use the All-In-One method of activation.

Tip: If your protection grid is more permanent you could bury the four stones at the corners of your property. Or they could also be placed under the floorboards.

Crystals Used:

4 Large Black Tourmaline Crystal Points
1 Large Red Tiger's Eye

Location Crystal Grid

Sacred Geometry Meaning:

The Square creates strong energetic boundaries. The Cross gives protection from all directions.

(1) Outer Support Stones: Black Tourmaline

In position 1 place four large Black Tourmaline Crystal Points in the four corners of your Home, property or room. Have them standing up if possible or pointing outwards. Black Tourmaline is highly protective and absorbs negativity. These crystals can be substituted for Tourmalinated Quartz Crystal Points, Shiva Lingams or Black Obsidian Crystal Points. You could also use four Black Obsidian Arrowheads, pointing outwards.

(2) Inner Support Stone: Red Tiger's Eye

For position 2 place a medium to large Red Tiger's Eye (also known as Dragon's Eye) near the front door. This needs to be just within your main entrance and ideally visible when you stand on the door step looking in. You could use a large Tumble Stone or any of the forms used for the Central Stones. This stone can be substituted for regular Tiger's Eye, Lapis Lazuli or a Shiva Lingam if not already used in the grid.

Intention Statement:

"I program this Crystal Grid to protect my .... and all who live here from all forms of harm.".

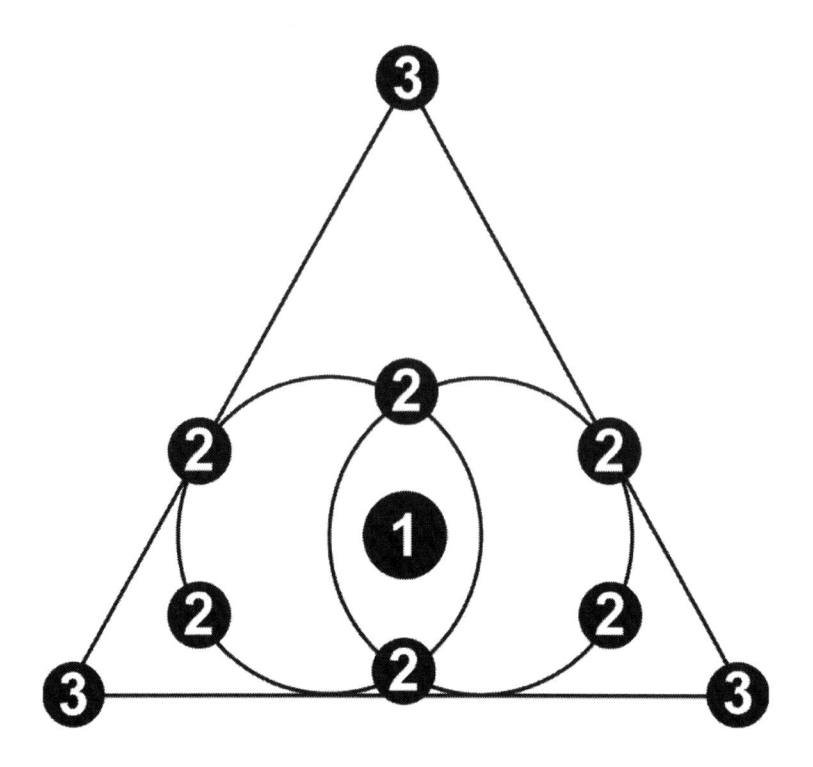

INCREASED ENERGY CRYSTAL GRID

This Regular Crystal Grid can be used to boost your energy. Use this grid when you are low on energy or when you have lots to do and need extra stamina and energy. It can help increase your energy levels or those of someone else that lacks energy. Write an affirmation of your intention on a small piece of paper. Fold this and place it under the Central Stone. You could also place a photo of another person who requests help with the note under the Central Stone.

Tip: For best results wear red Garnet jewellery or carry this energising stone with you at all times.

Crystals Used:

1 Large Clear Quartz
6 Carnelian Tumble Stones
3 Garnet Crystals or Tumble Stones

Regular Crystal Grid Template: I

Sacred Geometry Meaning:

The Triangle raises energy. The Vesica Piscis brings renewal.

(1) Central Stone: Clear Quartz

In position 1 place a large Clear Quartz crystal. Clear Quartz amplifies energies and expands the Aura. This crystal can be substituted with a Tangerine Quartz or Sunshine Aura.

(2) Inner Support Stones: Carnelian

In position 2 arrange the six Carnelian Tumble Stones. Carnelian increases energy levels. These crystals can be substituted with Tiger's Iron or Red Tourmaline.

(3) Outer Support Stones: Garnet

In position 3 arrange the three red Garnet Crystals or Tumble Stones. The fiery Garnets further boost energy. These crystals can be substituted with Red Tiger's Eye (also known as Dragon's Eye) or Rubies.

Intention Statement:

"*I program this Crystal Grid to boost .... energy levels*".

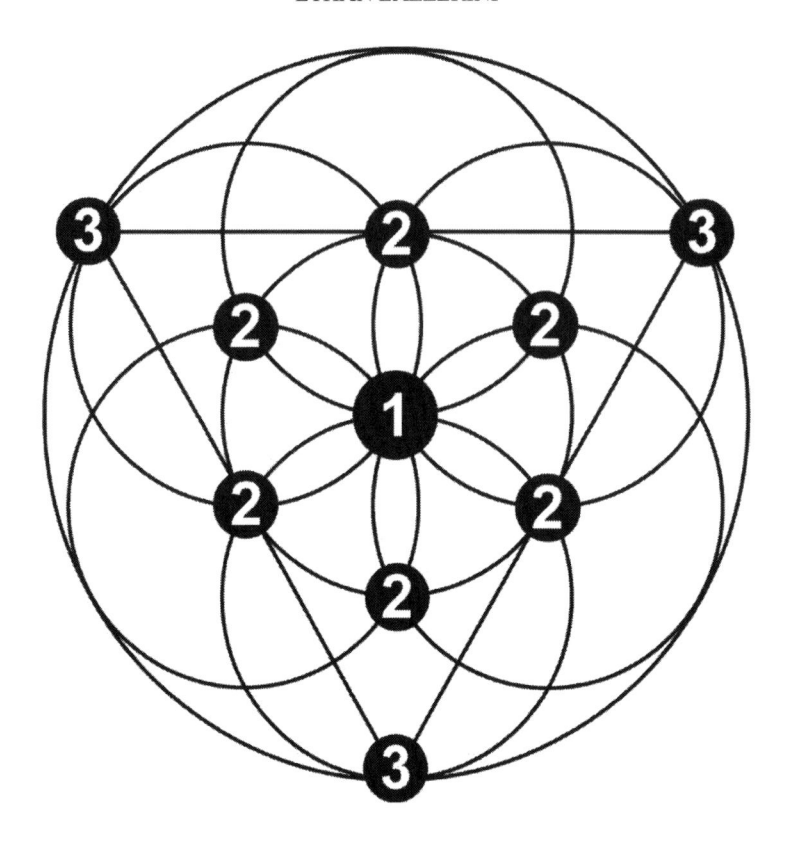

INSPIRATION & IDEAS CRYSTAL GRID

This Regular Crystal Grid can be used to bring new ideas and quick inspiration. Use this grid when you begin a creative project or need to think of one. It is ideal for times when you are all out of ideas. These crystals help you access information from your Higher Self. Write an affirmation of your intention on a small piece of paper. Fold this and place it under the Central Stone.

Tip: See if you can incorporate some crystal Pyramids into this design. A Quartz Crystal Point with a Phantom formation or Diamond Window facet will also work well here.

Crystals Used:

1 Large Clear Quartz
6 Labradorite Tumble Stones
3 Lapis Lazuli Tumble Stones

Regular Crystal Grid Template: G

Sacred Geometry Meaning:

The Seed of Life is for creativity and new beginnings. The Triangle boosts creativity and brings divine inspiration.

(1) Central Stone: Clear Quartz

In position 1 place a large Clear Quartz crystal. Clear Quartz channels inspiration and spiritual downloads. This crystal can be substituted with any Phantom Quartz, Chevron Amethyst (also known as Banded Amethyst or Dream Amethyst), Sodalite or Flame Aura (also known as Titanium Aura Quartz).

(2) Inner Support Stones: Labradorite

In position 2 arrange the six Labradorite Tumble Stones. Labradorite stimulates creative ideas. These crystals can be substituted with Chevron Amethyst or Selenite.

(3) Outer Support Stones: Lapis Lazuli

In position 3 arrange the three Lapis Lazuli Tumble Stones. Lapis Lazuli brings inspiration. These crystals can be substituted with Sodalite, Selenite or Flame Aura if not used already. If using Crystal Points, have them pointing inwards.

Intention Statement:

"I program this Crystal Grid to bring me inspiration and creative ideas".

KARMA RELEASE CRYSTAL GRID

This Regular Crystal Grid can be used to work through and release old karma. Use this grid to help resolve repeating patterns in situations or relationships. This purifying lotus flower helps you move on from troublesome relationships, taking with you only the lessons learned. You will still need to take steps towards resolving conflicts or breaking negative habits. Write an affirmation of your intention on a small piece of paper. Fold this and place it under the Central Stone.

Tip: For the Central Stone you could use a Crystal Flame to transmute negative energies or a Merkaba to accelerate growth.

Crystals Used:

1 Large Lapis Lazuli
3 Celestite Tumble Stones
3 Sugilite Tumble Stones
9 Tibetan Black Quartz Double Terminated Crystals

Regular Crystal Grid Template: J

Sacred Geometry Meaning:

The Seed of Life is for personal growth and a fresh start. The Enneagram is for completion, compassion and peace.

(1) Central Stone: Lapis Lazuli

In position 1 place a large Lapis Lazuli crystal. Lapis Lazuli is good for karma release work. This crystal can be substituted with a Phantom Quartz Crystal Point, Angel Aura or Selenite.

(2) Inner Support Stones: Celestite

In position 2 arrange the three Celestite Tumble Stones. Celestite (also known as Celestine) clears karma and outdated past life vows. These crystals can be substituted with Angelite, Lithium Quartz or Aquamarine.

(3) Inner Support Stones: Sugilite

In position 3 arrange the three Sugilite Tumble Stones. Sugilite transmutes karmic energies. These crystals can be substituted with Amethyst. If using points, have them pointing outwards.

(4) Outer Support Stones: Tibetan Black Quartz

In position 4 arrange the nine Tibetan Black Quartz crystals, pointing outwards. Tibetan Black Quartz (also known as Tibetan Quartz) transmutes karma. These crystals can be substituted with Selenite or Clear Quartz, pointing outwards.

Intention Statement:

"*I program this Crystal Grid to resolve and release me from all karma associated with .... if that be for the highest and greatest good of all concerned*".

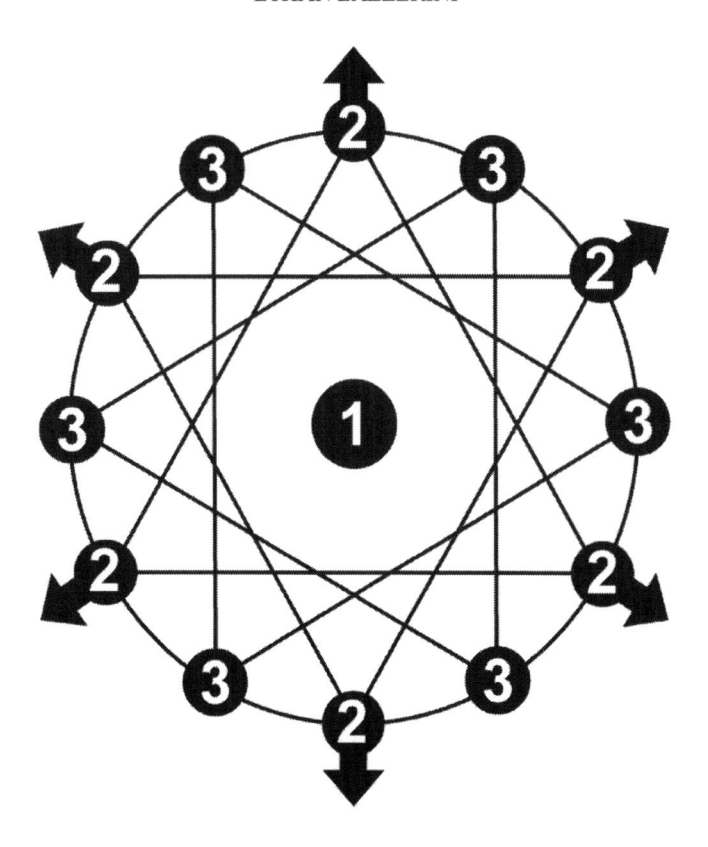

LIFE PURPOSE CRYSTAL GRID

This Regular Crystal Grid can be used to help you discover your life purpose. This is an important role or a career you came here to do in this lifetime. Use this grid to receive intuitive messages, guidance or signs relating to your life purpose. Allow this faceted diamond grid to align your life path with your higher purpose. Write an affirmation of your intention on a small piece of paper. Fold this and place it under the Central Stone.

Tip: For the Central Stone a Quartz Crystal Point with a Phantom formation or Diamond Window facet will further help connect you with your higher self.

Crystals Used:

1 Large Clear Quartz Crystal
6 Danburite Crystal Points
6 Amazonite Tumble Stones

Regular Crystal Grid Template: K

Sacred Geometry Meaning:

The Dodecagram aligns you with your destiny and life purpose. The Circle brings focus and celestial support.

(1) Central Stone: Clear Quartz

In position 1 place a large Clear Quartz crystal. Clear Quartz brings in spiritual wisdom. This crystal can be substituted with a Chevron Amethyst (also known as Banded Amethyst or Dream Amethyst), Golden Healer Quartz or Celestial Aura (also known as Tanzine Aura or Indigo Aura).

(2) Support Stones: Danburite

In position 2 arrange the six Danburite Crystal Points, pointing outwards. Danburite aligns you with your life purpose. These crystals can be substituted with Celestial Aura Crystal Points or Herkimer Diamonds.

(3) Support Stones: Amazonite

In position 3 arrange the six Amazonite Tumble Stones. Amazonite removes blocks and fear relating to your life purpose. These crystals can be substituted with Smoky Quartz. If using Crystal Points, have them pointing outwards.

Intention Statement:

"I program this Crystal Grid to help me discover and align with my divine life purpose".

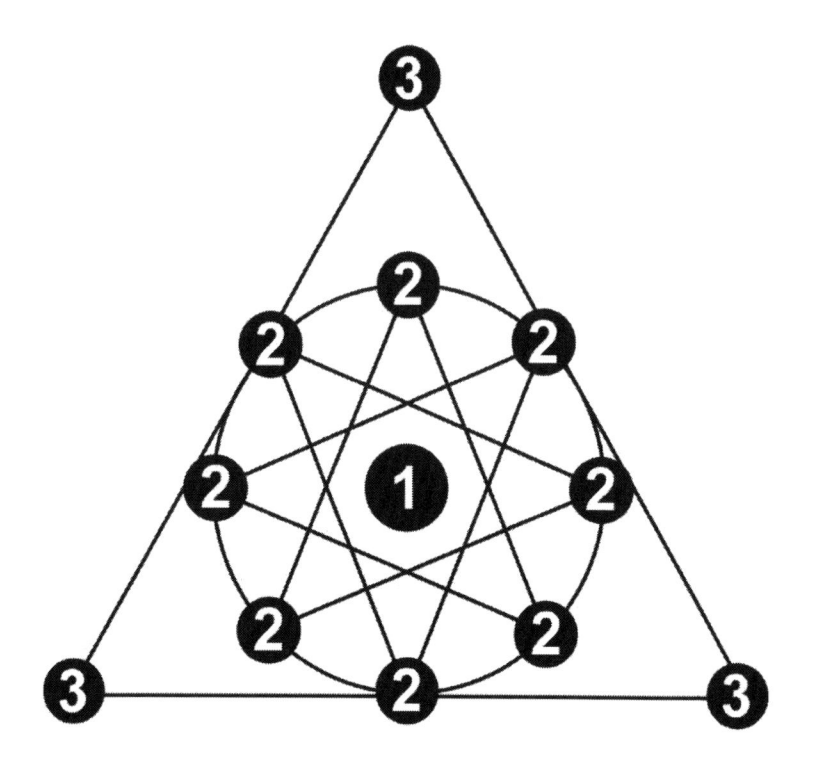

MOTIVATION CRYSTAL GRID

This Regular Crystal Grid can be used to boost motivation. Use this grid to help you start and complete projects. This grid is a good choice if you are procrastinating over something. These crystals will help support you as you take action steps towards your goals. The grid can be used for new projects or to complete an old one. Write an affirmation of your intention on a small piece of paper. Fold this and place it under the Central Stone.

Tip: Crystal Points, Crystal Pyramids and Crystal Flames make good choices for the Central Stone in this grid. They help raise the energy needed to get things moving.

Crystals Used:

1 Large Clear Quartz Crystal
8 Garnet Crystals or Tumble Stones
3 Carnelian Tumble Stones

Regular Crystal Grid Template: L

Sacred Geometry Meaning:

The Triangle raises energy. The Octagram increases determination and the Circle brings commitment.

(1) Central Stone: Clear Quartz

In position 1 place a large Clear Quartz crystal. Clear Quartz amplifies energies. This crystal can be substituted with a Hematoid Quartz or Tangerine Quartz crystal.

(2) Inner Support Stones: Garnet

In position 2 arrange the eight Garnet crystals or Tumble Stones. Red Garnet boosts energy and motivation. These crystals can be substituted with Tiger's Iron, Ruby or Red Tourmaline.

(3) Outer Support Stones: Carnelian

In position 3 arrange the three Carnelian Tumble Stones. Carnelian empowers and motivates. These crystals can be substituted with Bronzite or Mahogany Obsidian Tumble Stones or Arrowheads, pointing outwards.

Intention Statement:

"I program this Crystal Grid to boost my motivation, so that I can .... ".

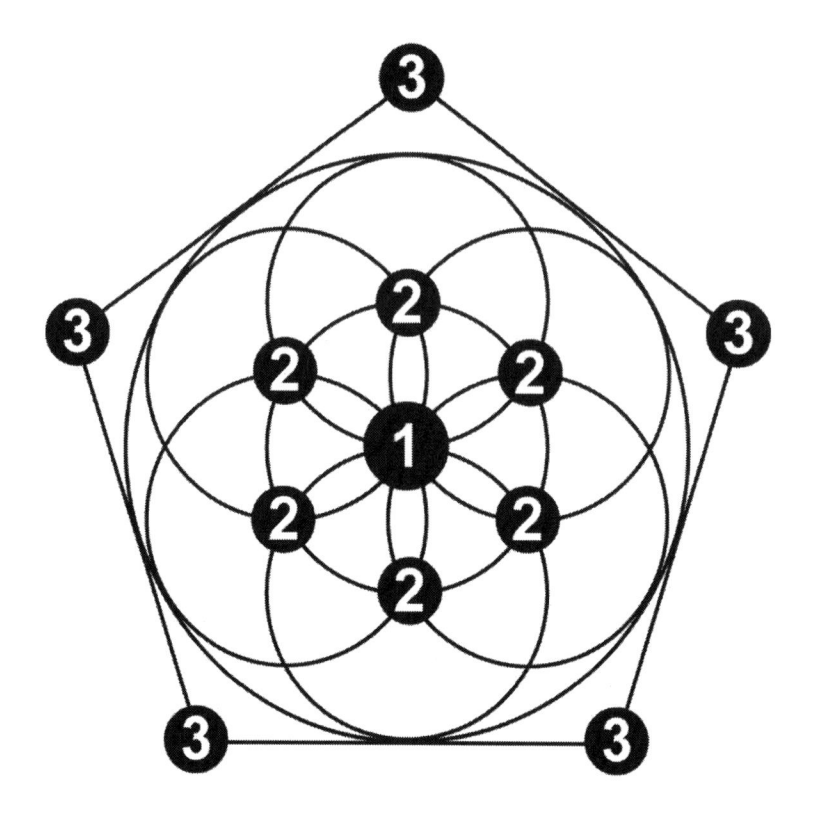

NEW BEGINNINGS CRYSTAL GRID

This Regular Crystal Grid can be used when you are looking for a fresh start. Use this grid to help you with new projects or making big life changes. You can use this grid during personal transitions and when taking brave new steps in your life. Write an affirmation of your intention on a small piece of paper. Fold this and place it under the Central Stone.

Tip: You could also place a small card or printed image of the Hindu deity Ganesh under your Central Stone. The elephant headed Ganesh or Ganesha is the opener of doors and the remover of obstacles.

Crystals Used:

1 Large Amazonite
6 Labradorite Tumble Stones
5 Celestite Tumble Stones or Crystal Points

Regular Crystal Grid Template: M

Sacred Geometry Meaning:

The Pentagon is for freedom and change. The Seed of Life is for new beginnings.

(1) Central Stone: Amazonite

In position 1 place a large Amazonite crystal. Amazonite helps in creating a fresh start. This crystal can be substituted with a Tangerine Quartz or a Clear Quartz crystal.

(2) Inner Support Stones: Labradorite

In position 2 arrange the six Labradorite Tumble Stones. Labradorite helps with life transitions. These crystals can be substituted with Fluorite or Healer's Gold (also known as Apache Gold).

(3) Outer Support Stones: Celestite

In position 3 arrange the five Celestite Tumble Stones or Crystal Points, pointing outwards. Celestite (also known as Celestine) helps navigate new chapters in our life. These crystals can be substituted with Moonstone, Lemon Chrysoprase (also known as Citron Chrysoprase) or Clear Quartz. If using Crystal Points, have them pointing outwards.

Intention Statement:

"I program this Crystal Grid to support and guide me to bright new changes in my life".

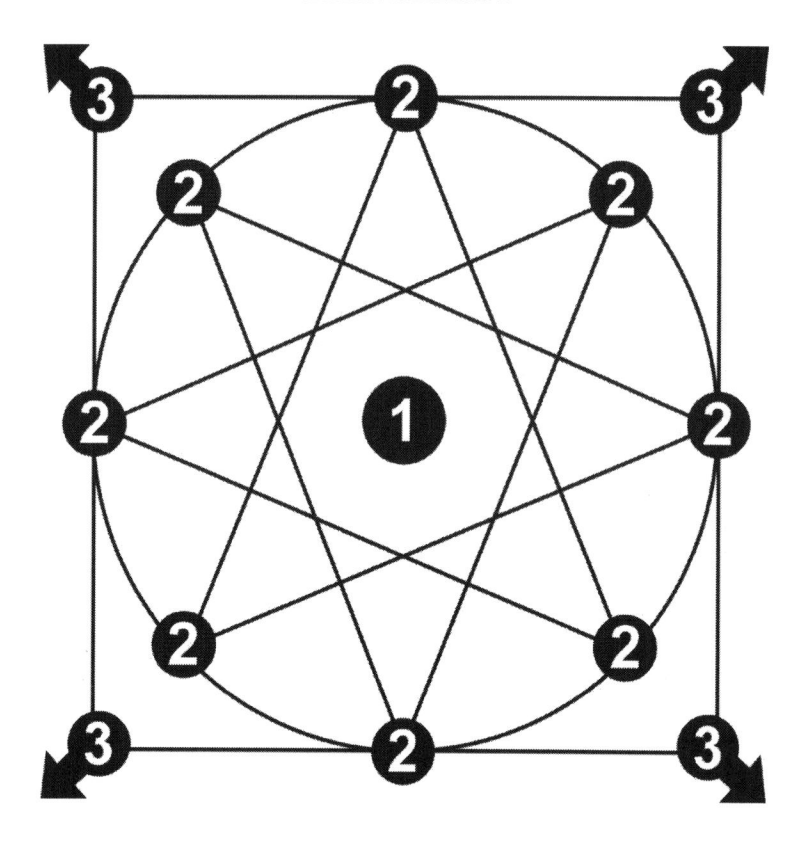

OVERCOME OBSTACLES CRYSTAL GRID

This Regular Crystal Grid can be used to overcome obstacles. Use this spinning cart wheel to break through stubborn blocks to goals, ambitions or any situation. These barriers can be lifted, help may appear or new paths around walls could be created. Write an affirmation of your intention on a small piece of paper. Fold this and place it under the Central Stone.

Tip: You could also place a small printed image of the Hindu deity Ganesh under your Central Stone. The Elephant headed Ganesh or Ganesha is the opener of doors and the remover of obstacles.

Crystals Used:

1 Large Mahogany Obsidian
8 Bronzite Tumble Stones
4 Clear Quartz Crystal Points

Regular Crystal Grid Template E

Sacred Geometry Meaning:

The Square brings inner strength and endurance. The Circle is for commitment and focus. The Octagram builds determination and brings success.

(1) Central Stone: Mahogany Obsidian

In position 1 place a large Mahogany Obsidian crystal. Mahogany Obsidian helps bulldoze obstacles out of the way. This crystal can be substituted with an Aragonite Star Cluster (Brown), Tangerine Aura crystal or Ammolite (Iridescent Ammonite).

(2) Inner Support Stones: Bronzite

In position 2 arrange the eight Bronzite Tumble Stones. Bronzite gives determination and confidence. These crystals can be substituted with Tiger's Eye or Tiger's Iron.

(3) Outer Support Stones: Clear Quartz

In position 3 arrange the four clear Quartz Crystal Points, pointing outwards. Clear Quartz focuses and amplifies the energies and intention.

Intention Statement:

"I program this Crystal Grid to remove and dissolve all obstacles in the way of me .... if that be for the highest and greatest good of all".

PEACE & HARMONY CRYSTAL GRID

This Regular Crystal Grid can be used to bring peace and harmony. Use this nine petaled lotus flower to calm inharmonious situations. It will help bring a peaceful energy back into your life or environment. This grid can be created after a very bad argument or series of clashes. Write an affirmation of your intention on a small piece of paper. If this situation involves your family or a relationship, you could also add a photo taken during happier times. Place these under the Central Stone.

Tip: Burn some lotus incense sticks to quickly purify and uplift the energy of your living space.

Crystals Used:

1 Large Amazonite
6 Green Jade Tumble Stones
9 Blue Lace Agate Tumble Stones

Regular Crystal Grid Template: F

Sacred Geometry Meaning:

The Enneagram supports unity and peace. The Flower of Life brings balance and harmony.

(1) Central Stone: Amazonite

In position 1 place a large Amazonite crystal. Amazonite brings peace. This crystal can be substituted with Rose Quartz or Clear Quartz.

(2) Inner Support Stones: Green Jade

In position 2 arrange the six Green Jade Tumble Stones. Green Jade brings peaceful energies. These crystals can be substituted with White Jade, Green Aventurine, Turquoise or Larimar (also known as Dolphin Stone).

(3) Outer Support Stones: Blue Lace Agate

In position 3 arrange the nine Blue Lace Agate Tumble Stones. Blue Lace Agate supports harmonious communication. These crystals can be substituted with Angelite, Rhodonite or Clear Quartz Crystal Points, pointing outwards.

Intention Statement:

"I program this Crystal Grid to restore peace and harmony to .... if that be for the highest and greatest good of all concerned".

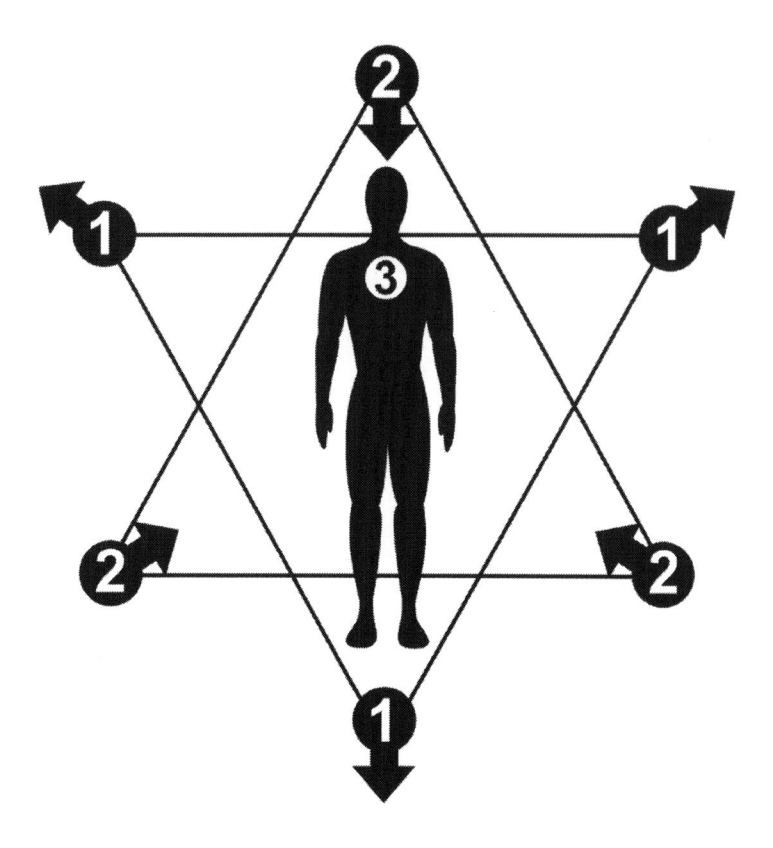

PERSONAL HEALING CRYSTAL GRID

This Body Crystal Grid layout is used for supporting health and healing. It will draw out stagnant energies and bring in healing energy. Use this healing star when you are ill or recovering from an illness. You can also use this grid when you feel run down or your immune system is weak. This Crystal Grid can be used every day for as long as is needed to help restore health and balance your energy. Use the All-In-One method of activation.

Tip: When selecting the Tumble Stone for the Heart Chakra position, choose one that is flat on one side so that it will not move when placed on your body.

Crystals Used:

3 Smoky Quartz Crystal Points
3 Clear Quartz Crystal Points
1 Amazonite Tumble Stone

Body Crystal Grid

Sacred Geometry Meaning:

The Star of David balances spiritual and physical energies.

(1) Support Stones: Smoky Quartz

In position 1 arrange three Smoky Quartz Crystal Points, pointing outwards. Smoky Quartz grounds you and absorbs negative energies. These crystals can be substituted with Black Tourmaline Crystal Points or Citrine.

(2) Support Stones: Clear Quartz

In position 2 arrange three Clear Quartz Crystal Points, pointing inwards. Clear Quartz brings in healing energy and expands the Aura.

(3) Chakra Crystal: Amazonite

Lay down within the grid. In position 3 place the Amazonite Tumble Stone over your Heart Chakra. This is in the middle of your chest area. Amazonite is healing and balances energies. This crystal can be substituted with Turquoise, Faden Quartz or Lapis Lazuli.

Close your eyes and take some deep breaths. Lay here for about 10 to 15 minutes. Take your time before getting up again.

Intention Statement:

"I program this Crystal Grid to heal me and balance my energies on all levels".

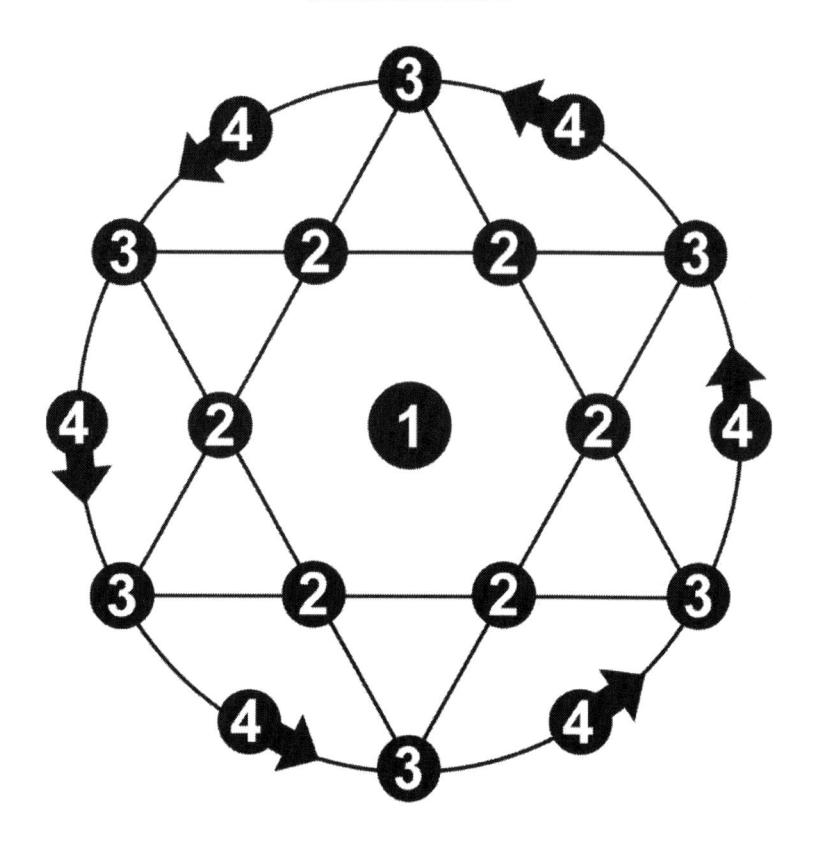

PROTECTION CRYSTAL GRID

This Regular Crystal Grid can be used for spiritual and psychic protection. Use this grid to protect yourself, your family, loved ones or someone else. This army of crystals will shield and protect you from all forms of harm. If protecting someone else or your family, you could also add a photo. Place this with your note. Write an affirmation of your intention on a small piece of paper. Fold this and place it under the Central Stone.

Tip: For the Central Stone you could use a Crystal Merkaba, Crystal Egg, Crystal Angel or Crystal Laughing Buddha.

Crystals Used:

1 Large Hematite
6 Black Obsidian Tumble Stones
6 Lapis Lazuli Tumble Stones
6 Amethyst Crystal Points

Regular Crystal Grid Template: N

Sacred Geometry Meaning:

The Star of David is for spiritual support and protection. The Circle creates an energetic boundary or psychic shield.

(1) Central Stone: Hematite

In position 1 place a large Hematite crystal. Hematite protects and strengthens your Aura. This crystal can be substituted with Smoky Quartz, Aqua Aura or Clear Quartz.

(2) Inner Support Stones: Black Obsidian

In position 2 arrange the six Black Obsidian Tumble Stones or Arrowheads, pointing outwards. Black Obsidian is highly protective. These crystals can be substituted with Black Onyx or Apache Tears.

(3) Outer Support Stones: Lapis Lazuli

In position 3 arrange the six Lapis Lazuli Tumble Stones. Lapis Lazuli gives spiritual protection. These crystals can be substituted with Red Tiger's Eye (also known as Dragon's Eye) or golden Tiger's Eye.

(4) Outer Support Stones: Amethyst

In position 4 arrange the six Amethyst Crystal Points, pointing anticlockwise. Amethyst is for psychic protection and transmutation. These crystals can be substituted with Black Tourmaline Crystal Points.

Intention Statement:

"I program this Crystal Grid to protect .... from all forms of harm".

PSYCHIC ATTACK SHIELD CRYSTAL GRID

This Body Crystal Grid layout can be used if you are experiencing a psychic attack. Activate this emergency shield of protection if you sense that someone is sending you harmful thoughts or energies. The crystals will shield you from the negative energies and break the connection. Repeat as and when needed. If the situation is ongoing, use one of the other more permanent protection grids in this book. Use the All-In-One method of activation.

Tip: Wear Hematite jewellery for at least the next 24 hours.

Crystals Used:

6 Large Hematite Tumble Stones
6 Black Tourmaline Double Terminated Crystal Points

Body Crystal Grid

Sacred Geometry Meaning:

The Star of David and Hexagon brings spiritual protection.

(1) Support Stones: Hematite

In position 1 arrange six large Hematite Tumble Stones. Hematite brings strong protection and strengthens your Aura. These crystals can be substituted with Aqua Aura or Red Tiger's Eye (also known as Dragon's Eye).

(2) Support Stones: Black Tourmaline

In position 2 arrange six Black Tourmaline Double Terminated Crystal Points. Black Tourmaline is protective and absorbs negative energies. These crystals can be substituted with Double Terminated Smoky Quartz or Tibetan Black Quartz Double Terminated Crystals (also known as Tibetan Quartz). If only single terminated points are available, have them pointing anticlockwise. You can also use Black Obsidian Arrowheads, pointing in an anticlockwise direction.

Sit within this grid for at least 15 minutes to half an hour. Take some deep breaths and try to relax. Visualise yourself inside a large metallic sphere of Hematite. Take your time before getting up again.

Intention Statement:

"I program this Crystal Grid to become an impenetrable shield of protection and to block all forms of harm, now!".

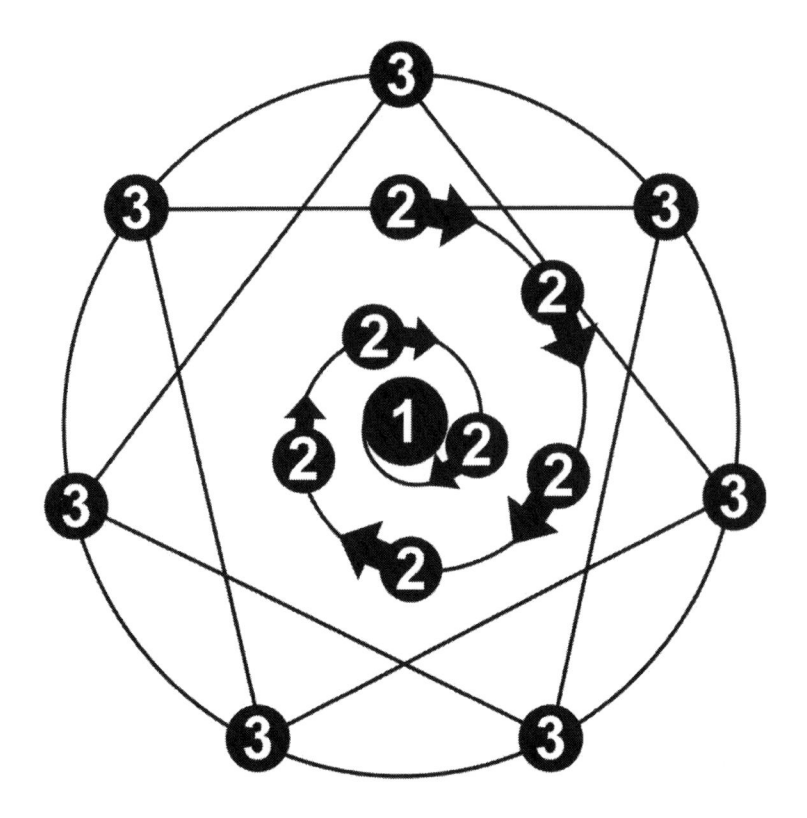

PSYCHIC DEVELOPMENT CRYSTAL GRID

This Regular Crystal Grid can be used to help you develop your psychic abilities or intuition. Use this mystical grid to increase your sense and awareness of subtle energies. This Crystal Grid should be used in conjunction with psychic development exercises and study. Write an affirmation of your intention on a small piece of paper. Fold this and place it under the Central Stone.

Tip: You could use a Crystal Sphere for the Central Stone to further focus the energies of your Third Eye Chakra. Or use a Crystal Merkaba for spiritual growth.

Crystals Used:

1 Large Amethyst
7 Clear Quartz Crystal Points
7 Rainbow Moonstone Tumble Stones

Regular Crystal Grid Template: O

Sacred Geometry Meaning:

The Septagram brings spiritual knowledge. The Circle is for focus and protection. The Spiral is for spiritual development and inner guidance.

(1) Central Stone: Amethyst

In position 1 place a large Amethyst crystal. Amethyst accelerates psychic development. This crystal can be substituted with Chevron Amethyst (also known as Banded Amethyst or Dream Amethyst), Aqua Aura or Clear Quartz.

(2) Inner Support Stones: Clear Quartz

In position 2 arrange the seven Clear Quartz Crystal Points pointing clockwise where you wish along the spiral. Clear Quartz brings clear intuitive messages.

(3) Outer Support Stones: Rainbow Moonstone

In position 3 arrange the seven Rainbow Moonstone Tumble Stones. Rainbow Moonstone (also known as White Labradorite) is good for intuition and psychic development. These crystals can be substituted with regular Moonstone, Sodalite or Lapis Lazuli.

Intention Statement:

"I program this Crystal Grid to help me develop my psychic abilities and receive clear intuitive insights".

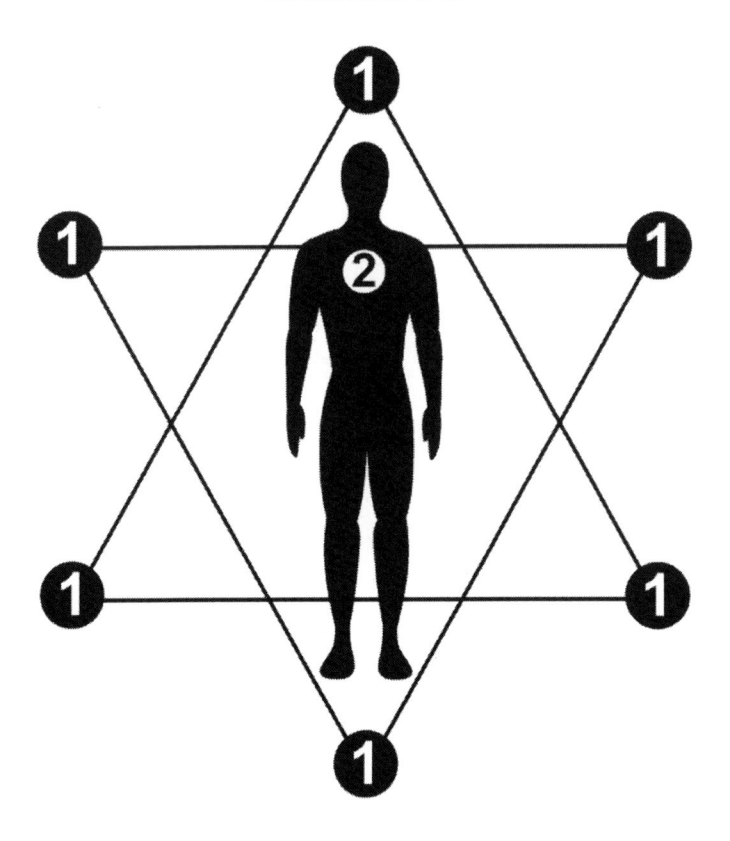

SELF LOVE CRYSTAL GRID

This Body Crystal Grid layout is used for developing greater self love. This pink rose will help heal the emotional body and integrate a better connection with the physical body. The crystal placed on the chest opens and clears the Heart Chakra. This personal healing Crystal Grid can be used every day or as and when you feel you need it. It should be used in conjunction with incorporating regular self care habits and 'me time' into your life. Use the All-In-One method of activation.

Tip: Heart shaped crystals could be used as the Central Stone or any of the Support Stones if you like.

Crystals Used:

6 Rose Quartz Tumble Stones
1 Rhodochrosite Tumble Stone

Body Crystal Grid

Sacred Geometry Meaning:

The Star of David integrates spiritual and physical energies. It is also an ancient symbol of the Heart Chakra.

(1) Support Stones: Rose Quartz

In position 1 arrange six Rose Quartz Tumble Stones. Rose Quartz heals the heart. These crystals can be substituted with Mangano Calcite or Pink Opals.

(2) Chakra Crystal: Rhodochrosite

Lay down within the grid. In position 2 place the Rhodochrosite Tumble Stone over your Heart Chakra. This is in the middle of your chest area. Rhodochrosite deeply clears the Heart Chakra and helps develop self love. This crystal can be substituted with Rhodonite, Chrysocolla or Amazonite.

Close your eyes and take some deep breaths. Lay here for about 10 to 15 minutes. Take your time before getting up again.

Intention Statement:

"*I program this Crystal Grid to heal my heart and develop greater self love*".

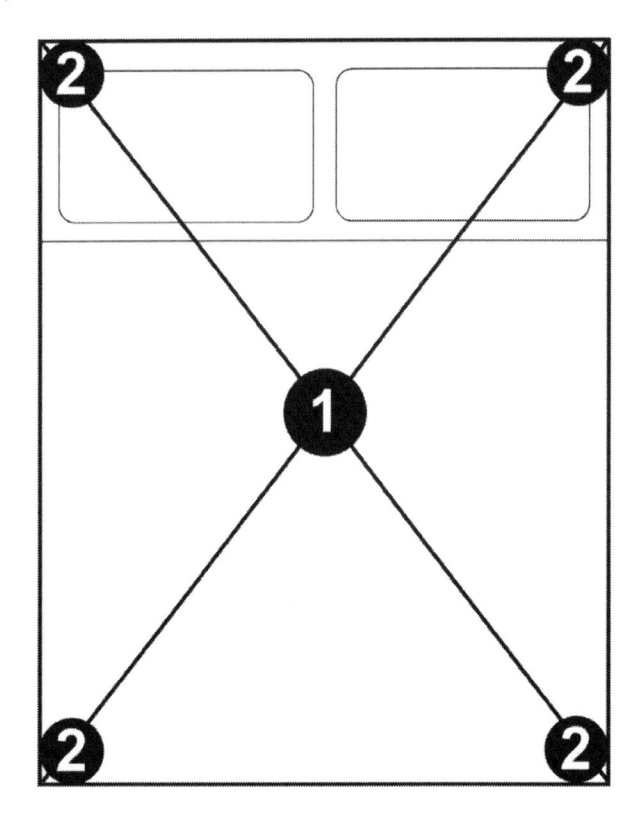

SLEEP WELL CRYSTAL GRID

This Location Crystal Grid can be used to support a better night's sleep. The crystals in this grid create a soothing and grounding energy that is more conductive to sleep. The crystals will need to be cleansed on a regular basis to work at optimal levels. I recommend once a week or at least once a month. If placing crystals under a mattress please place something soft and protective around them to avoid damage. Use the All-In-One method of activation.

Tip: Avoid using Crystal Points or Pyramids, which may be too energising for the sleep area. Try to use smooth rounded shapes like Tumble Stones, Crystal Eggs or Crystal Spheres.

Crystals Used:

1 Large Hematite
4 Medium Rose Quartz Tumble Stones

Location Crystal Grid

Sacred Geometry Meaning:

The Square creates a supportive and protective environment. The Cross helps integrate and balance the physical and spiritual bodies.

(1) Central Stone: Hematite

In position 1 place a large Hematite crystal under the bed. Remember to use only smooth and rounded crystal forms or a Tumble Stone. Hematite will keep your energy grounded and protected during sleep. This crystal can be substituted for Red Jasper, Black Tourmaline or Smoky Quartz.

(2) Support Stones: Rose Quartz

In position 2 place four medium to large Rose Quartz Tumble Stones under the bed or mattress. These crystals can be substituted for Turquoise or Howlite.

Intention Statement:

"I program this Crystal Grid to give me a deep, peaceful and restorative nights sleep".

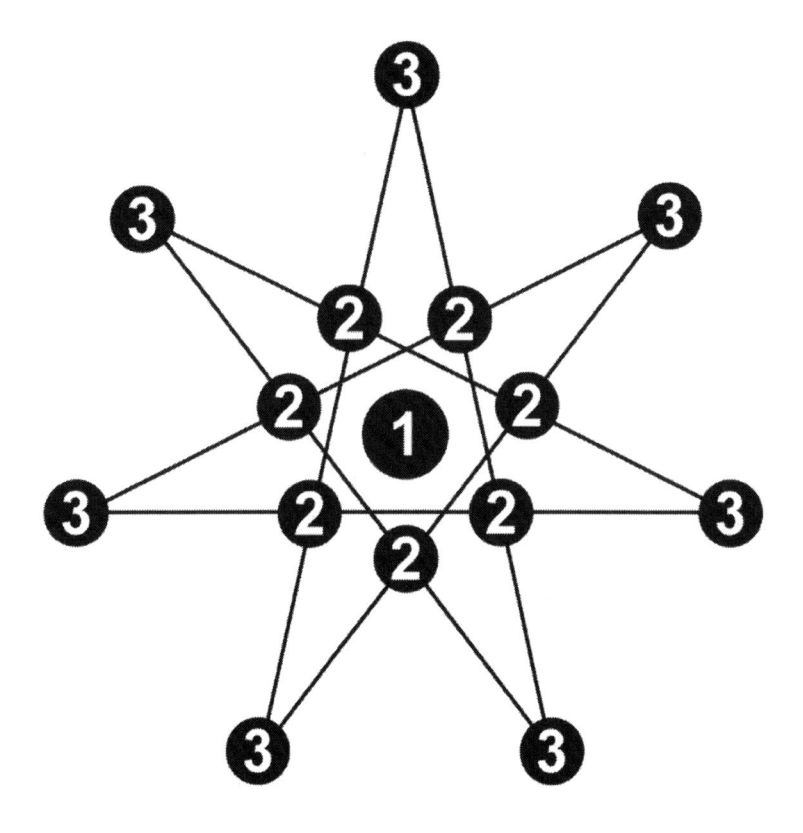

SPIRITUAL GUIDANCE CRYSTAL GRID

This Regular Crystal Grid can be used to receive spiritual guidance. Use this mystic star to receive messages and signs from the Universe or your guides, as to the next steps in your life. Guidance may come in the form of intuitive knowing, synchronicity, dreams, helpful people or information you come across in books or online for example. Write an affirmation of your intention on a small piece of paper. Fold this and place it under the Central Stone.

Tip: You could use a Standing Crystal Point or a Crystal Pyramid for the Central Stone to act like a beacon tower.

Crystals Used:

1 Large Clear Quartz
7 Lapis Lazuli Tumble Stones
7 Amethyst Tumble Stones

Regular Crystal Grid Template: P

Sacred Geometry Meaning:

The Septagram brings spiritual knowledge and wisdom.

(1) Central Stone: Clear Quartz

In position 1 place a large Clear Quartz crystal. Clear Quartz brings clear insights and spiritual downloads. This crystal can be substituted with Chevron Amethyst (also known as Banded Amethyst or Dream Amethyst).

(2) Inner Support Stones: Lapis Lazuli

In position 2 arrange the seven Lapis Lazuli Tumble Stones. Lapis Lazuli enhances intuition and spiritual connection. These crystals can be substituted with Sodalite, Moonstone or Rainbow Moonstone (also known as White Labradorite).

(3) Outer Support Stones: Amethyst

In position 3 arrange the seven Amethyst Tumble Stones. Amethyst is used for spiritual connection. These crystals can be substituted with Herkimer Diamonds or Chevron Amethyst if not used already.

Intention Statement:

"I program this Crystal Grid to help me receive spiritual guidance about ....".

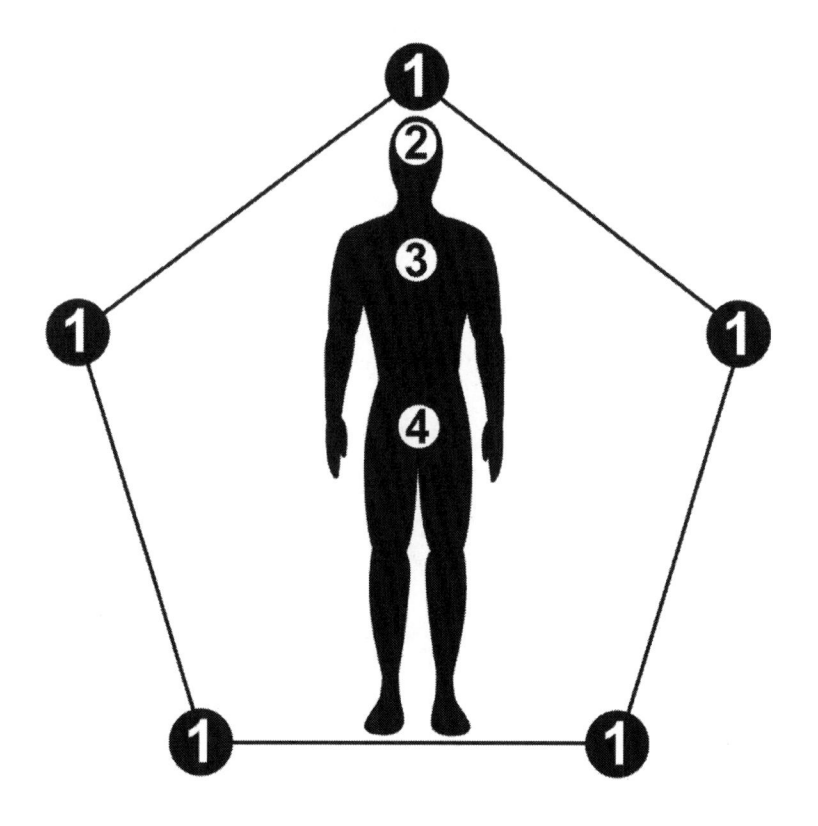

STRESS RELIEF CRYSTAL GRID

This Body Crystal Grid layout can be very helpful for reducing stress. The grid can be set up at the end of a stressful day or when you are knee deep in a stressful time in your life. This special stress busting grid can be customised to treat three different types of stress. You can select one, two or three of the Chakra Crystals depending on your current situation and type of stress you are experiencing. Use the All-In-One method of activation.

Tip: You could store these crystals all together in a drawstring bag or small box for easy access, whenever you are going through a stressful time.

Crystals Used:

5 Amazonite Tumble Stones
1 Turquoise Tumble Stone
1 Rose Quartz Tumble Stone
1 Shiva Lingam

Body Crystal Grid

Sacred Geometry Meaning:

The Pentagon brings freedom and renewal.

(1) Support Stones: Amazonite

In position 1 arrange five Amazonite Tumble Stones. Amazonite helps bring balance and melts stress away. These crystals can be substituted with Howlite, Infinite or clear Quartz Crystal Points, pointing outwards.

(2) Chakra Crystal: Turquoise

Lay down within the grid. If you are experiencing **mental stress** in position 2 place a Turquoise Tumble Stone over your Third Eye Chakra. Substitute with Howlite.

(3) Chakra Crystal: Rose Quartz

If you are experiencing **emotional stress** in position 3 place a Rose Quartz Tumble Stone over your Heart Chakra. This is in the middle of the chest area. Substitute with Rhodochrosite.

(4) Chakra Crystal: Shiva Lingam

If you are experiencing **work related or financial stress** in position 4 place a Shiva Lingam stone over or under your Root Chakra. At the base of your spine. Substitute with Red Jasper.

Close your eyes and take some deep breaths. Lay here for about 15 to 20 minutes. Take your time before getting up again.

Intention Statement:

"I program this Crystal Grid to dissolve all stress from my body and Aura".

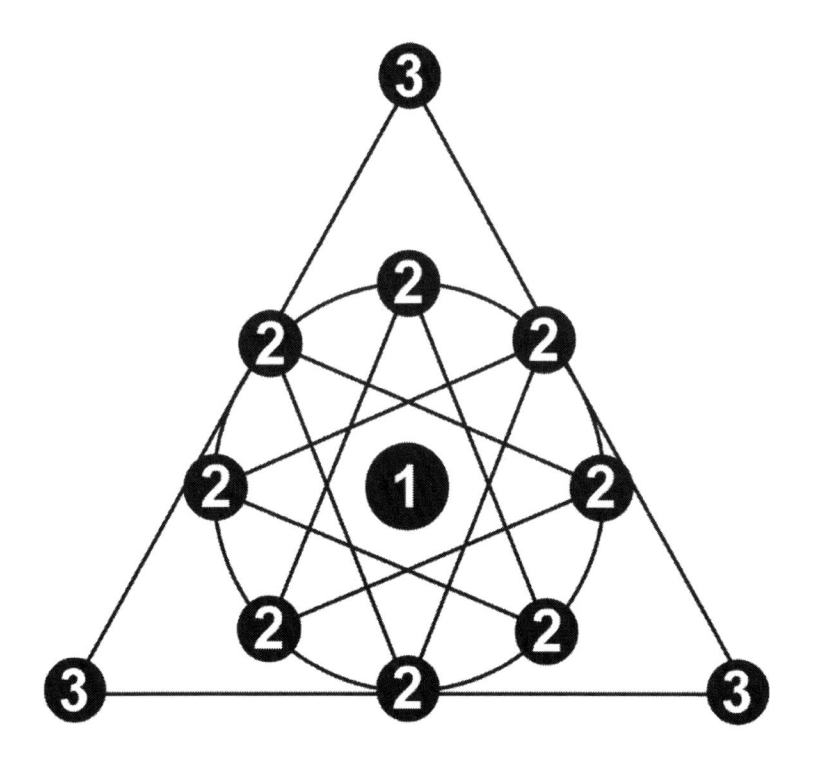

SUCCESS CRYSTAL GRID

This Regular Crystal Grid can be used to improve your chances of success. Use this golden pyramid to help a project or goal become successful. Allow this grid to armor yourself with the determination to make it happen. It assists you in pushing forward with your goals, empowering yourself and overcoming challenges. Write an affirmation of your intention on a small piece of paper. Fold this and place it under the Central Stone.

Tip: You could also place a Lucky Chinese Coin on top of the folded note to attract wealth and prosperity. These are antique or replica coins with a square hole through the middle. Always place these with the four characters side face up.

Crystals Used:

1 Large Tiger's Eye
8 Mahogany Obsidian Tumble Stones
3 Citrine Tumble Stones

Regular Crystal Grid Template: L

Sacred Geometry Meaning:

The Octagram is for success and determination. The circle is for focus and commitment. The Triangle is for manifestation.

(1) Central Stone: Tiger's Eye

In position 1 place a large Tiger's Eye crystal. Tiger's Eye brings self confidence, faith and success. This crystal can be substituted with Citrine or Clear Quartz.

(2) Inner Support Stones: Mahogany Obsidian

In position 2 arrange the eight Mahogany Obsidian Tumble Stones or Arrowheads, pointing outwards. Mahogany Obsidian helps overcome obstacles. These crystals can be substituted with Aragonite (Brown), Tangerine Aura or Bronzite.

(3) Outer Support Stones: Citrine

In position 3 arrange three Citrine Tumble Stones. If you want to use Citrine Crystal Points instead, have them pointing outwards. Citrine attracts success and supports manifesting. These crystals can be substituted with Pyrite, Green Jade or Yellow Jade.

Intention Statement:

"I program this Crystal Grid for success with .... if that be for my highest and greatest good and the highest and greatest good of all".

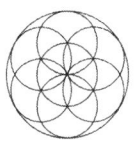

10

CREATING YOUR OWN CRYSTAL GRIDS

Once you have tried a few of the Crystal Grids featured in this book you may want to start creating your own. Perhaps you want to create a Crystal Grid for a specific need not covered here? Or one of the grids is not exactly what you're looking for. Maybe you want to create a Crystal Grid by only following your intuition on the arrangement and selections of stones.

Crystal Grids can be made by anyone and although you can just follow your intuition with creating them, I do think a combination of head and heart will get you more predictable results.

There are an infinite number of ways to combine Sacred Geometry with crystals. We are blessed to live on a Planet with an abundance of natural minerals. There are many other crystals I could have used in the grids in this book. There is more than one way to make a cake and it is the same with Crystal Grids.

In this chapter I will show you how I put my Crystal Grids together, so that you have a process to follow or a guide to base your own formula on. Then just use your intuition and inner knowing on deciding what will work best for your grids.

Set Your Intention

The seed of all Crystal Grids is their intention. Start by thinking about exactly what it is that you want your grid to do. You could use a note pad or journal to focus on something you want to manifest or do with your grid. If you can summarise this into less than a few words, it will bring greater focus and clarity.

This will be the title for your Crystal Grid. When you record your Crystal Grid, you want a name that makes it instantly clear what it was made for so that you can use it again in the future. This is also a good point to use these words to create an intention statement. You will use this when you activate the Crystal Grid and if you are including a note under the Central Stone.

Explore Crystal Options

Next make a list of crystals you could include in your Crystal Grid. Do not try to be perfect, you just need a list of possible crystals you could use for this particular grid. You need the crystals to all be in alignment with your grid's purpose.

If you have a good knowledge of Crystal Healing, you may know which crystals you could use. Otherwise use trusted and recommended sources such as books about the properties of different types of crystals. Use the index of a good book to find crystal suggestions for your intention. Search by the main intention of your grid and any related keywords. Think about the qualities you would need to achieve your goal and then list the crystals that support these qualities.

Other factors you need to consider are rarity, price and availability. Some crystals are expensive or rare. These can sometimes be okay for a Central Stone. When it comes to multiple Support Stones, some options may just not be possible. There are also some crystals that you will never see in larger forms, suitable for Central Stones or gridding your House.

Choose Your Geometric Shapes

Before you make your final selection of stones you should also think about the geometries you are going to use. For this you can refer to the Sacred Geometry Reference Guide at the beginning of this book. You may also wish to study books on Sacred Geometry and symbols. My quick reference guide was designed to summarise the key properties and uses of these symbols to make this really easy for you.

Just like selecting crystals, you want to harness the energies of geometric shapes, which will support the intention of your Crystal Grid. As you come across shapes that have meanings that relate to your Crystal Grid, note them down or draw a little sketch of them. You should have a few possible shapes you could use in your grid. The Star of David and the Flower of Life are so universal that they will be possible options for most grids.

Design Your Crystal Grid

Once you have looked at all the options, circle any shapes that you think suit your grid the best. You may be able to use just one geometric shape or consider combining two or even three. Take your pen and try to draw different ways to combine the shapes. Try overlaying them or placing one shape inside the other. Eventually you will create something that just jumps off the page and feels right. Circle or highlight your final chosen design.

If you're creating a Regular Crystal Grid you will want to mark the location where the Central Stone will sit. This is usually in the exact centre of most geometric shapes. I draw a small circle or put a large dot here.

Most geometric shapes have corners and intersection points, which you can place other crystals. There are usually at least two areas where a group of Support Stones can be placed. If you look at the grids in this book, you can see most grids have a group of Inner Support Stones and Outer Support Stones. Where you place these crystals is up to you but try to go with what feels and looks right. You may only wish to work with one group of crystals. Once you have decided where the Support Stones should go, mark these points off with smaller circles or dots.

Select Your Central Stone

This should be a crystal that represents your core intention, the main purpose of your grid. Because this crystal needs to be bigger, you may find that the crystals on your list may not always be suitable. In this case I would use Clear Quartz as this can be used for any Central Stone.

Once you have chosen your Central Stone write this on your diagram next to the circle or dot in the central part of your grid. Or you can draw an arrow pointing to the location. Now the only thing left to do is choose the form of your Central Stone. My list of recommended Central Stones will help you. You can of course use other shapes not listed in this book.

Select Your Support Stones

These crystals should also represent the intention behind your Crystal Grid or supporting qualities, which are related to the main purpose. This may include other properties, which will assist you in reaching your goal, or bring in additional energies that will be beneficial to the desired result. Your grid may need one or two groups of Support Stones. If using more than one group, think about which crystals add properties that will help you.

These crystals can be Tumble Stones or in some cases small Crystal Points. You can also use more specialist shapes like spheres and pyramids if they are available and you are able to do so. What is more important is that you can find enough crystals to complete your grid. Look at your Crystal Grid plan and think about where you wish to place these stones. This is where your intuition will come into play. Imagine the crystals in a location around the grid. How does this feel?

If you already have some of the crystals you are considering, then you could even lay them out and plan your grids that way. There will be a combination that just seems to fit. Mark your final selections down on your diagram.

Consider How The Energy Flows

One last thing that you will have to consider if you create your own Crystal Grids is energy flow. Wherever you place Crystal Points or other geometric crystal shapes, you are channeling energies in different ways and directions.

As explained earlier Crystal Points direct energies, so if you use them think carefully about how you will point them. Generally most Crystal Points in a Crystal Grid will point outwards. This is based on the idea that you are sending energies out into the Universe for manifesting, releasing or sending healing for example. Inward pointing Crystal Points could be used to draw energies inward. This could be used in healing Body Crystal Grids or when increased energy is needed. In Location Grids you may wish to bring positive energies into your Home for example.

Crystals can also be placed to create a circuit such as in a circle. I find this is useful if you want to create some kind of continuous supply or for a protective shield. This type of arrangement can either build up energy like a vortex or create a wall of energy. Your intention will be the key here as always. As a general rule place Crystal Points pointing in a clockwise direction for attracting something or building energy. You could point the crystals in an anticlockwise direction for releasing, breaking an energetic connection or protection.

Putting It All Together

Once everything is planned and ready, you can cleanse and consecrate the crystals or any additional items. Then activate and arrange your Crystal Grid in your preferred way.

If all of this seems like too much work, don't worry. I wrote this book to give you lots of ready made grids, which can be altered and customised as you wish. If you want more grids, let me know and I may just write a second volume...

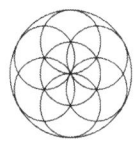

11

TROUBLESHOOTING

Crystals Grids are a tool for manifesting and creating change. As with all manifestation methods, sometimes things do not work out exactly as planned or not at all. There are reasons why this can happen and I want to address these in this chapter. If you have created a Crystal Grid and have yet to see the results or feel the effects of it yet, see if any of the below could be the reason and find out what to do about it.

Divine Timing

This is something that applies to any spiritual work or manifestation technique. Often people give up on something or say that something they tried to make happen did not work. You need to give your Crystal Grid time to work. Things will not just fall out the sky just because you ask. Fruit takes time to grow and ripen.

Your desire sometimes will take longer than you would like. If it is something big or life changing, events may need to happen to allow it to manifest. Often you will get everything you need but just not exactly when you want it. Things may turn up later down the road and usually only when you are ready. Sometimes we can ask for things that at the time we ask could actually cause more problems for us.

We may have to go through situations or experiences, which are far more important to us and our personal growth. This is often not evident at the time and can only be understood in hindsight. Try to have faith that what you want is on its way.

Negative Thinking & Limiting Beliefs

Having negative thoughts throughout your day is normal. Doubts in your goals and dreams are part of the human experience. That being said, excessive negative thinking and worries can bring your vibration down. Manifesting something positive in this state of mind and energy is not very easy.

Sometimes we learn limiting beliefs from our family, society, the media and through experiences we had when we were younger. These negative beliefs can stay with us our whole life if you don't learn how to spot them. Try to be honest with yourself. Do you have any limiting beliefs about the intention behind your Crystal Grid?

Your Crystal Grid is doing its thing, but if you are putting up a constant black cloud over your head, you may be creating your own road blocks. There are many methods to help you develop a more positive and success drawing mindset. If this sounds like something you have a problem with, look into ways to think more positively.

There is no quick fix for this but awareness of your thoughts and emotions is the best place to start. Consider daily meditation, affirmations, mindfulness, hypnosis or any number of self help books we have available to us now. Carrying or wearing Smoky

Quartz or Snowflake Obsidian daily can also be helpful to absorb negative energies and thoughts.

Are You Taking Action?

Remember the Crystal Grid Diamond at the beginning of this book? The central facet was action. This may not always be something that you can take action on but most often there are things you could do. Explore what other people do in your situation or even better those who have overcome it. How can you increase your chances of success? What can you do on a consistent or daily basis? Perhaps it is time you changed your actions and tried a new method. It is all about showing the Universe or anyone else involved that you really want this.

How's Your Sacred Space?

Have you been taking good care of your crystals and Crystal Grid since you set it up? Is it covered in dust? You must keep the area where the grid is placed and the crystals free of dust. Remember dust is like stagnant energy, it slows things down. Make sure you dust your grid regularly to keep the energies fresh and alive.

The other thing you need to consider is anything that is placed close to your Crystal Grid. Is there a pile of newspapers or magazines nearby? Boxes of junk or a project that you have since abandoned or keep putting off? Watch for electrical items or even other crystals too. Other crystals placed close to the grid could interfere with the energy and flow of your grid. Remove or move these objects to another location and see if things improve. Test things to rule out these possible issues.

Cleanse The Crystal Grid Again

Both the energy of the room you have placed your Crystal Grid plus the grid itself, will need cleansing from time to time. I recommend once a month. You can use the Universal White Light method for cleansing explained earlier. The easiest way to cleanse a grid and the room is with sacred sound or incense. You could use smudging or some other cleansing incense like Palo Santo, Sandalwood, Camphor, Copal or Frankincense and Myrrh.

Or use a Tibetan Singing Bowl or Ting Shas, the small brass Buddhist cymbals. Your grid may have absorbed some negative energies from your worries or fears, which could be blocking the crystals from working at their best.

Tweaking Your Crystal Grid

Occasionally some of the crystals in a grid are just not right for you. Perhaps you chose one of the crystals because it was the only one you had. Or the crystal you wanted was not available at the time. Perhaps another crystal will work better for you? Sometimes even the form or shape of the crystal just needs changing to get things moving.

Select another crystal option or substitute stone from this book or if you know of a stone that you feel is more suitable for you personally, use that. If you know how to use a pendulum, you could dowse to find the best crystal for you. You can either reprogram and activate the grid again or just do this for the new crystals. Crystals that are removed will need to be cleansed and deprogrammed of course.

You may just want to add something to the Crystal Grid. This could be extra Quartz Crystal Points to further focus and amplify the energies of the grid. Or it may be the inclusion of a photo, printed image or some other symbolic item.

Note the change you made and the date you added or replaced the crystals or items. Give any tweaks like this some time to see changes. If nothing happens differently you may want to try grid reactivation as a last resort.

Consider Grid Reactivation

If you have tried all of the methods above, you may wish to reprogram and reactivate your Crystal Grid. Sometimes especially when we are new to programming crystals, our minds get too caught up in doing everything right that we don't really connect with the crystals well. This will take time and practice to feel more natural.

By starting again with your crystals you get to do everything again and hopefully in a much more relaxed and focused state of mind. Were you happy with the wording of your statement of intention and note if you used one? Consider revising it and get really clear. A lack of clarity can bring unclear results.

Remove all the crystals, cleanse and deprogram them so that you are starting with a clean slate. Try and activate your grid when you are feeling relaxed and not rushed or stressed. To help you can burn some lavender essential oil and meditate for a while before you begin.

If you are empathic or worried about energies from the day interfering with the process, cleanse your Aura. You can use visualisations to do this or use the Aura Clearing Crystal Grid included in this book. Another easy way to do this is to visualise a shower of cosmic silver white light raining down over and through you. Allow this cosmic energy shower to cleanse your Aura for around two to three minutes or until you feel it has been done.

Chakra Clearing

As well as keeping your Aura clear of the energies of the day, you may want to cleanse your Chakras too. The Chakra System relates to all areas of your life, mindset, psychic energies and emotions. When your Chakras are out of balance or blocked they can inhibit your ability to attract positive things into your life. When they are clear your energy is clear and that clarity attracts things to you and helps you manifest what you need. Chakra clearing can be a very useful technique for spiritual growth, personal development and healing work. When your Chakras are kept clear, you will find you can manifest things quicker.

Here's a little secret you may not have heard before. It is a very good idea to cleanse and balance your Chakras before you activate your Crystal Grids. There are many ways to do this. Using Chakra Crystals is one of the easiest and most effective ways. If you want to learn more about this, you may be interested in my book **Crystal Healing For The Chakras**.

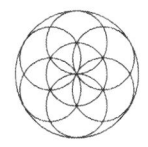

AFTERWARDS

Hopefully this book has given you a better understanding of the workings of Crystal Grids and Sacred Geometry. I hope this book will be a valuable go-to source for Crystal Grids whenever you need one. Using Crystal Grids is a useful tool to have on your journey with crystals and Crystal Healing. May they help amplify your intentions, open new doorways and bring blessings and positive change into your life.

If you enjoyed this book and found it helpful in any way, **please consider leaving me a short review on Amazon**. Your reviews are hugely helpful to me as an Independent Author and will help others be able to find this book in the search results.

Thank you for your support,

Ethan

ABOUT THE AUTHOR

Ethan Lazzerini is an author and blogger based in Yorkshire, England. He has been working with crystals for more than 25 years. Ethan works intuitively and practically with crystals to access the information and energy they hold. He believes crystals are spiritual tools and allies for personal development, spiritual growth, manifesting and psychic protection. In his books and popular blog articles, he aims to make Crystal Healing clear and easy to apply to everyday life.

When he is not writing, reading or hunting for crystals, he makes Crystal Healing jewellery for his successful jewellery line Merkaba Warrior. For lots of helpful Crystal Healing guides and tips, please visit his popular website and blog:

www.ethanlazzerini.com

Stay connected with Ethan Lazzerini on social media:

Facebook, Pinterest & Instagram

BIBLIOGRAPHY

Earth Grids: The Secret Patterns of Gaia's Sacred Sites
Hugh Newman

Gems in Myth, Legend and Lore
Bruce G. Knuth

Leys: Secret Spirit Paths in Ancient Britain
Danny Sullivan

Magic Stones: The Secret World of Ancient Megaliths
Jan Pohribny

Sacred Geometry
Miranda Lundy

The Ancient Secret of the Flower of Life: Volume 1
Drunvalo Melchizedek

The Element Encyclopedia of Secret Signs and Symbols
Adele Nozedar

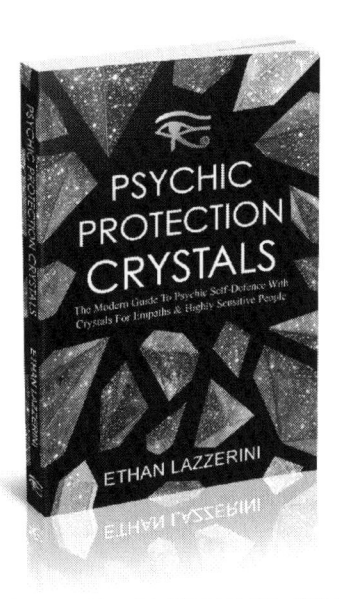

PSYCHIC PROTECTION CRYSTALS

The Modern Guide To Psychic Self-Defence With Crystals For Empaths & Highly Sensitive People

Do you take on the energy of others too easily? Are you constantly battling bad vibes? Have you ever experienced a psychic attack? In this book you will learn how to create strong and healthy energetic boundaries. Empower yourself with simple to advanced techniques to strengthen your aura and shield yourself from negative energies, toxic people and environments.

Meet the Guardians of the Mineral Kingdom. Explore over 50 crystals and their unique protective properties in detail. Supercharge your shielding, breeze past bad vibes and neutralise negative energies!

Available Now in Paperback & Kindle!

CRYSTAL HEALING FOR THE CHAKRAS

A Beginner's Guide To The Chakras & Chakra Balancing with Crystals

When your Chakras are clear your intuition is sharper, you can manifest things quicker and it awakens your psychic abilities. Learn how to tell when your Chakras are clear, balanced or blocked. Use my step-by-step techniques and simple meditations to cleanse, balance and align all your Chakras with crystals.

Beautifully illustrated with full colour photos and suitable for beginners and beyond. This book takes you further than the traditional seven Major Chakras. Discover the secrets of the Soul Star and Earth Star Chakras. Understanding the Chakra System can take your knowledge of crystals to the next level.

Available Now in Paperback & Kindle!

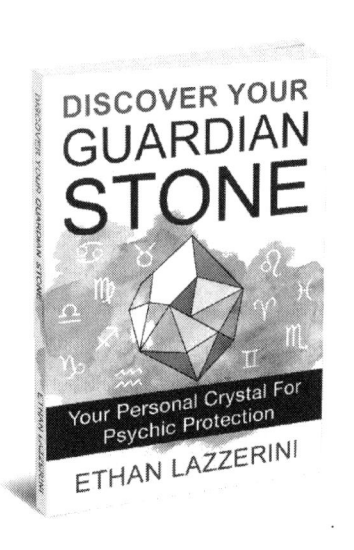

DISCOVER YOUR GUARDIAN STONE

Your Personal Crystal For Psychic Protection

If you subscribe to my monthly Crystal Newsletter and updates you will get this exclusive Ebook free. Learn how to use astrology to discover your personal go-to crystal for protection. Illustrated with full colour photos. This book is only available on my website by visiting the link below:

www.ethanlazzerini.com/freegift

Printed in Great Britain
by Amazon